S0-AGA-019

JUSTICE FOR TRUTH

J. D. MORRISON

Things are not always what they appear…

xulon
PRESS

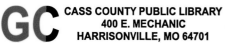

GC **CASS COUNTY PUBLIC LIBRARY**
400 E. MECHANIC
HARRISONVILLE, MO 64701

0 0022 0559450 6

Copyright © 2008 by J. D. Morrison

Justice for Truth
by J. D. Morrison

Printed in the United States of America

ISBN 978-1-60477-399-6

All rights reserved solely by the author. The author guarantees all contents are original and do not infringe upon the legal rights of any other person or work. No part of this book may be reproduced in any form without the permission of the author. The views expressed in this book are not necessarily those of the publisher.

Unless otherwise indicated, Bible quotations are taken from the New King James Version of the Bible. Copyright © 1979, 1980, 1982 by Thomas Nelson.

www.xulonpress.com

For Richie's honor

Dedicated to Dr. Kathy Newell:
Without you the purpose of Richie's death would have been left unfulfilled. We pass our strongest judgment on another human being when we decide whether or not they are worth our time. Thank you for believing Richie was worth your time.

*T*his story is completely true. Some names have been changed for privacy issues.

CONTENTS

ACKNOWLEDGMENTS

To Randy Wright:

Thank you for all the advice and encouragement you gave me in writing this book. I'm sorry that you weren't here to see the finished product. Most of all, thank you for being my friend. Rest in peace.

To "Wild Bill" (the blond one sitting next to the Mother):

Thank you for believing in Richie and for sticking with me when no one else would. You have given me new faith in the law profession.

To Lou Accurso (the flashy one):

If you ever bring suit against me, I will settle immediately. ☺

To Larry:

You are my rock. Thanks for putting up with my hibernating for days at a time in front of the computer. Your belief in me has fueled this effort. Thank you for listening to the voice that told you to go home that day.

To LaRetha, Shirley, Annette, Elaine, and DK:

Your input was invaluable. Without you this book would not have been nearly as readable.

Chapter 1

Point of Crisis

Idon't remember the weather that day. Or what I had for lunch. What important tasks I was performing at work that fateful day…I don't remember. The one inescapable memory of September 12, 2003, the one memory of which I would prefer a thousand deaths if I could rid myself, is the memory of my vibrant, young son's death rattle.

As history is partitioned into B.C. and A.D., every event mapped into my memory is now filed on one side or the other of *that* day. Like a huge novel pared by a single bookmark, the span of my life is likewise divided — by September 12, 2003.

Around 4:00 P.M. I responded to the second flashing light that was signaling my husband, Larry, trying to call in on a second line of my desk phone at work. I figured it must be urgent, so I pressed the button to place a business call on hold.

"Rich's work just called. He was supposed to have been there at noon, and I can't wake him up." His words pierced through the Friday afternoon malaise and triggered an instant rise of panic in my stomach.

"What do you mean, he's just being lazy and won't get up, or he's unresponsive?"

My son, Richie, a 23-yr-old college senior, wouldn't just not show up to his part-time job at our neighborhood grocery store. He liked it too much.

So my heart sank at Larry's reply. "Well yeah, like, unresponsive."

As I heard my mouth saying, "I'll be right there," I slammed down the receiver and dashed the two cubicle rows over to my boss's desk. I suppose the look on my face told her as much as my words.

"Cathy, I need to go home. My husband just called to say Richie's work phoned the house looking for him. He was scheduled to be there at noon today, and Larry can't wake him up."

"Go! Don't tell me, just go!" Cathy's words spun me toward the exit.

As a former nurse I should have immediately known to call 9-1-1 to send help to my son. Why didn't I?

Richie has always been such a sound sleeper, I reasoned with myself. And we had been up until after midnight the night before. Maybe he was just really tired. I was much more familiar with my son than was my husband of three years. I could more accurately assess the situation when I got there. And it just *had* to be OK.

I pressed the button to activate my emergency flashers as I pulled onto eastbound I-70 from downtown Kansas City, Missouri. One look ahead revealed that the rush-hour traffic had already begun to congest the choicest route home, so I steered my car onto Truman Road. I thought taking a back road would most likely be quicker at that time of day – probably a panic-induced miscalculation on my part.

As I began the 15-minute drive home that seemed to last an eternity, my mind was racing. *What is going on with Richie? What will I find when I get there? If it's really that bad, what will I do? Will I be able to handle it?*

As I crawled along Truman road, watching telephone poles creep by much too slowly, my hands began gripping the steering wheel ever tighter, my pulse and respiration rates steadily rising. *If only I had a cell phone to keep me connected to Larry.*

Eventually I made my escape from the prison of bumpers and accelerated toward the house. As I passed over a long rail bridge near the Missouri River, I suddenly became strangely in tune with the song that was flowing from the radio. Time and existence ceased. A slow, melodic – no, angelic – tune adhered to the words, "He'll be the peace that fills your soul; remember He is in control," filled the cabin around me. The dial was tuned to my usual station, but this was an artist and selection I had never before heard — and would never hear again.

Suddenly, with a jolt the real world closed back in. And nothing had changed. Except me. I was different. My spirit had relaxed into a mysterious repose.

I completed the journey home, and as I rushed through the front door I was met by Larry. Slinging my purse onto the kitchen table, I made a mad dash down the stairs into our finished, walkout basement where Richie was living while finishing his studies at DeVry University.

In my son's room I encountered a sight that is burned into my memory like a still from a morbid picture show. My days spent as a nurse gave me the wisdom to know that Richie was dying. I didn't know *why* he was dying, but I knew he was.

"Larry, help me get him onto the floor. I think we're about to have to do CPR!"

It's amazing how clearly the resuscitation procedures were in my head from nursing school all those years before. I remembered that chest compressions are best performed on a hard surface, but Richie was lying on his back in his soft bed.

We pulled back the covers and gently lowered him onto the floor as I watched him take what was to be one of his last voluntary breaths. As we placed his cyanotic body onto the carpet, we heard it — the death rattle.

I instructed Larry to give Richie a couple of rescue breaths as I dialed 9-1-1 from the phone on Richie's bedside stand – a phone that Richie and I had picked out together from Radio Shack just a few months earlier. I struggled to keep my emotions in check as I supplied information to the operator on the other end of the line. I stated that we had a 23-year-old male down, and then, as hastily as I could, I provided driving directions to our house.

"Does he have a history of heart problems?" I knew immediately where the operator's questioning was headed, so I moved to lead our conversation in a more accurate direction.

"No. None. He had a wreck yesterday, and I don't know if maybe that has something to do with it…"

My statement was cut short by more specific questioning about his condition.

"Is he breathing? Does he have a pulse?"

I couldn't feel a pulse in the carotid artery region of Richie's neck, and his respirations were infrequent, shallow gasps known in the medical world as agonal breathing. Then there was nothing.

With the operator's procedural instructions lending support, I began performing CPR– a skill I had acquired but had never actually performed on anyone other than the training dummy. And now I was having to perform it on the person to whom I was the closest in the entire world.

I had Larry verify that Richie's chest was rising as I placed my mouth over his and blew. It was. But I was getting no results. My son's condition was deteriorating by the second.

"God, we need some help here." My prayer was desperate.

I knew that Richie's life was hanging in the balance, and, being raised a Christian, I instinctively knew where to turn during such a crisis.

Exactly ten minutes elapsed between my 9-1-1 call and the medics arriving at Richie's side. I have never been more relieved to see anyone.

As they entered my son's small bedroom, I withdrew to the adjacent living area. I stationed myself so that I could observe the activity of those hovering around him, as I nervously conversed with a police officer that had just arrived at the scene. I recall naming for him the medications Richie regularly took.

"Zoloft and amoxicillin."

The remainder of the conversation is hazy, other than I think he asked me if Richie had been depressed lately. Richie had a history of anxiety and depression but had seemingly been doing quite well in the recent past, I told him. And I believe I repeated the fact that Richie had been involved in a wreck 24 hours before.

As precious minutes ticked by, I could see that the EMTs were still performing chest compressions on Richie. I knew the situation was becoming grave.

"Turn it for good, Lord, turn it for good." The prayer emanated from my lips, over and over, without any conscious effort on my part, birthed from a strong belief that God can transform any bad situation into a positive. And this was the absolute *worst* of situations.

I scurried back upstairs to the kitchen and grabbed the cordless phone from its base. My voice was so hysterical when my oldest sister, LaRetha, answered her phone in Holliday, Texas, that she initially was unable to recognize what I was saying or even who I was. Fortunately she had caller ID.

"LaRetha, pray! Pray! It's Richie! Something's wrong with him! He's dying! Richie's dying! They're having to do CPR on him!"

I frantically told her what little I was able to comprehend of what was happening. We then hung up so she could make calls to inform "the family," as Richie always called the close-knit circle of my mother and siblings. They would flood heaven with prayers for a child we all loved beyond description.

My one brother, SFC Larry Richard Morgan, was halfway to Atchison, Kansas, to check in for his Army National Guard drill when he got the news. He spontaneously turned his truck back toward Kansas City as his wife, Johnna, sped from their home ten minutes away. I met her on our front lawn.

As she and I leaned on each other, talking and praying, I caught a glimpse of the medics, accompanied by my husband, carrying Richie on a stretcher around the side yard to a waiting ambulance. Larry broke away and came over to inform us that they had finally re-established Richie's heartbeat even though he was still comatose. At least it was something. A sigh of release broke from my chest.

As the ambulance pulled away, the three of us quickly joined hands to form a circle. I once again prayed to the Great Author of Life that He would help us. And He did. Actually, He already had. In a most unusual way.

Chapter 2

A Bruised Reed

Richie Patterson was born not only from my body, he was born from my soul. I knew him. Do you understand? I *knew* him.

Explaining him is a different matter. He was a complex being with many facets, some of which were contradictory. He was at once timid and bold. Sweet and grumpy. Ambitious and lazy. Independent and needy. Sensitive and abrasive.

His uniqueness was manifested from birth. His intense cries as a tiny infant always gave the impression he was mad. He would hold his breath as he wailed until his face would start to turn a bluish color – a practice which always scared me half to death.

He was second in birth order, so I already had some mothering experience when he came along, but nothing I had seen from my firstborn, Hadley, prepared me to deal with Richie.

By his early childhood it had become clear that he was an intellectual genius. One of his favorite things to do was to sit quietly in the company of adults and listen – just listen. He had a hunger for knowledge and was fascinated by anything that was a mental challenge. Conversely, he was less than impressive at physical conquests, though he did develop into one of the team's most consistent hitters the year he played baseball. He never hit a homerun, but you could almost always count on him to make it safely to first base.

He didn't make many friends, and the ones he made were extremely close. Casual friendships were of no use to him; he wanted to know and be known. His strong sense of justice fed a palpable disdain for bullies. His words were measured more in quality than quantity, and he never had any interest in softening the blow. You knew where you stood with Richie Patterson.

It wasn't until age eleven that his anxiety disorder was correctly diagnosed. All the symptoms had been there along the way but had somehow been missed – which meant he had endured many miserable medical procedures in an attempt to determine the etiology of his poor bladder and bowel control up through the early elementary grades. The inevitable teasing that came from his classmates drove him inward and resulted in agonizing shyness and gnawed-to-the-blood fingertips.

What finally exposed the truth of his condition was when a continual forced, dry cough was incorrectly diagnosed as asthma. When severe chest pain caused by bronchodilators induced a visit to an ear, nose, and throat specialist for allergy identification, the new doctor gave Richie a thorough examination...and, his voice filled with urgency, he implored me to get Richie to a child psychologist right away. Richie's cough had absolutely nothing to do with a respiratory condition, he explained.

Richie began seeing the therapist weekly, and I removed him from public school and began teaching him at home. I became his protector. It was a period of exceptional bonding for the two of us.

The therapist began by working with Richie on techniques to combat the insomnia that had plagued him as long as anyone could remember. She gradually gained his trust and pressed on to deeper issues. Richie's primary torment came from knowing nothing of his father, she had ascertained. I should at least show Richie a picture of him, she told me. I'm embarrassed to say I didn't have one.

Richie was born to a two-time loser. With the first pregnancy I could claim youthful ignorance and find some sense of redemption. But when I was carrying Richie, I was so overwhelmed by shame that I have often wondered if maybe my self scorn somehow seeped through the wall of my womb to infect his forming substance.

I was apprehensive as I dialed his father's number, as I was aware that Mike Patterson was now married, and he and his wife, Jackie, had been blessed with two young children of their own. Some awkward and painful days ensued after I made my request for a photograph, but, due mostly to the fact that Jackie Patterson is an angel, Richie gradually forged a relationship with his Dad — and he adored his new stepmother and half-siblings, Aja and Seth. Richie was delighted when Mike and Jackie's final child, Caleb, was born. Richie was mesmerized by Caleb's sweet innocence.

Time spent in the Pattersons' home was always a treat for Richie. Two things always came out when he returned from there – first, that it was neat for him to experience how a nuclear family functioned, and second, how amazed he was by Jackie's acceptance and tenderness toward him. "And she has every reason to hate me," he would say.

Richie struggled with the fact that he had been the product of a mistake. He felt like he was damaged goods, like God must be scrambling to come up with a Plan B in order to figure out some use for him.

By the time he reached the age to enter high school he felt that he was ready to face the public system again. So, after jumping through some hoops to get them to receive him back from home school, he was enrolled.

It was during his freshman year in high school that we moved from Comanche, a tiny rural town in southern

Oklahoma, to the Kansas City area. It was a big change for Richie, but one he embraced. He liked the anonymity of the enormous Shawnee Mission, Kansas, school system; he could fade into the crowd without much notice, a nice fit for his shyness. And he loved the energy and the amenities of the city.

He quickly found a best friend in RJ Lansing. Richie and RJ spent so much time in each other's homes that RJ's mother and I both felt as though we had an additional son. For a time Mrs. Lansing even stocked her refrigerator with Richie's favorite drink — Coca-Cola.

RJ and Richie were what I lovingly call computer nerds, and they were both nocturnal, sitting up for countless marathon sessions into the wee hours of the morning trying to best each other at some virtual or video game, breaking only for runs to the local Steak and Shake or Taco Bell for a snack. They spent much of their time together bent double in laughter at something funny – or something they could *make* funny with their dry wit.

When Richie was eighteen, he discovered that an old kindergarten classmate from Comanche was currently living just on the other side of Kansas City. After exchanging a few e-mails with her, he nervously phoned and asked her out for what would be his first ever date. Even though nothing became of the relationship, I was pleased to see his confidence.

Life sailed along for Richie, with a 4.0 GPA, until a year or so into his college days at DeVry University. I made a fateful decision that would impact his life more than I ever imagined — I met and married Larry Morrison, who relocated us to the east side of Kansas City, into the state of Missouri. My marriage left Richie feeling like an outsider. That same summer Richie's younger brother, Quentin, had also gotten married, and he and his wife, Tiffany, chose to stay on the west side of the city. Hadley had long since been living in Texas, and we were more than 400 miles away from Richie's Dad. When RJ headed off to a university in another city with a steady girlfriend on his arm, Richie found himself feeling acutely alone.

The old anxiety demon that had tortured Richie as a child reared its ugly head again. Richie reached out for his Dad, with whom he had enjoyed much less contact after we had left Oklahoma, and he spoke of his anguish to our family doctor, who prescribed him Paxil. His grades went into a freefall, and he quit a good job without giving proper notice. He confided to me that he felt the Paxil wasn't working for him – he said he felt disconnected from the world, like he didn't and couldn't care about anything, so he quit taking it.

He moved in with his Uncle Larry Richard, who had just gone through a divorce, thinking they might be good support for each other. Richie seemed to be making an effort to learn how to be a man, how to make his own way in the world, but he struggled with being separated from the only security he had known. So, like the broken lamb, he returned to the shepherdess.

My husband, Larry, went out of his way to make Richie feel comfortable in our home, but it just wasn't the same. I had depended on Richie for many things during the years I had raised him. Now he erroneously felt that I didn't need him anymore. He was joyous that I had found someone that cared for me, but he felt awkward living in another man's home. So, despite our many trips out for meals and movies, just the two of us, he felt deserted.

In February 2002, at the end of trimester, just 22 hours shy of graduation, he pulled out of DeVry in order to save what little GPA he had left. During his final term there he had found a new friend named Matthew Morrison. But Matthew was graduating, and that would remove the only pleasantry Richie still found in dragging himself to school each day, plus Matthew was moving to Philadelphia to begin a new life – another disappointment for Richie.

One night, trying to lose himself, he climbed into his old 1989 Mazda and started driving. And he didn't stop driving until he was in the largest metropolis in the country, New York City, which is halfway across the United States. By the time he called home for help, his feet were bleeding from miles of walking, which had caused blisters to pop. He hadn't comprehended the steep parking rates of New York City. When he had returned to retrieve his car from a lot where he had left it, he didn't have the required funds. Nor did he have enough money to get himself a motel room. Larry and I spent a harrowing night finding a way to channel enough cash to him to sustain him while he reclaimed his car and made the long trip back to Kansas City. I also notified his Dad and Jackie.

When Richie got home he was ashamed and embarrassed for having put us through the ordeal. The ever-compassionate Jackie, who worked for an MD, suggested to Richie that he needed to try another antidepressant. She mentioned Zoloft might work better for him than the Paxil had — so he made another trip to our family doctor. Within a couple of weeks, the Zoloft had in fact seemed to start helping.

Richie knew he needed to find a career, but he was burnt out on school, and since he needed to pay back an enormous amount of student loan debt, he decided the military might solve both problems at once. He signed on with the U.S. Navy, and on April 18, 2002, he left for Basic Training in Great Lakes, Illinois.

I was excited when his first letter arrived. In spite of my being gravely ill with clinical depression at the time, I wrote him every couple of days. I told him how proud I was of him. He responded by declaring his determination to make me and the family proud and to regain his self-respect.

Unfortunately, he had feared the military would reject him if he were taking Zoloft, so he had ceased his prescription before talking to the recruitment officer. This made it hard for him to cope with the flare-up of an old back injury he had sustained while working in bygone years as a sorter for UPS…and with the Navy forcing him out with a medical discharge.

He returned home in June 2002 with a remnant of pneumonia he had contracted during his short stint as a sailor. As soon as he got well enough, he went to stay in Gilmer, Texas, with my sister, Cheryl, for a few weeks, to try and sort things out. Cheryl is a wise counselor, and she made Richie feel comfortable as he poured out his heart to her.

As summer 2002 inched into fall, he accepted an invitation from Matthew Morrison to move to Philadelphia and share an apartment with Matthew and another friend that had also graduated from DeVry. Richie was both excited and nervous. He had reservations about leaving the security of family again, plus he didn't have a job awaiting him in Philadelphia, but Matthew allayed his fears by predicting he would find something quickly once he got there. So, after receiving my blessing and help packing, he gave me a hug and headed toward a new adventure.

Finding a job was much more difficult for Richie than Matthew had assumed, however, especially since Richie didn't yet have a degree. After several weeks of knocking on doors, Richie finally ended up making sandwiches in a little shop called Saladworks – much more humbling than his previous jobs. But at least he had a job, and he was elated.

Richie and I stayed close through e-mails and my care packages to him. And he became a student in the school of life. He learned how difficult it was to make ends meet. He began to realize how hard it had been for me to be a single mother, and he apologized frequently for having begged for things he now realized I hadn't been able to afford as he was growing up. I could tell that my little boy was becoming a man.

Chapter 3

Healing Love

K ansas City International Airport was a swell of holiday travelers on December 20, 2002. I elbowed my way through the masses, searching for a single face. At last I saw Richie's familiar little half-smile coming toward me. We met with a warm, enfolding hug.

This was going to be an amazing Christmas. Not only was Richie coming in from Philadelphia, but I had just received my first grandbaby into the world three months earlier, on September 11; Quentin and Tiffany had a new daughter, Olivia. I had gone out and bought loads of greenery and decorations, complete with a beautiful lighted angel to adorn the top of the fresh-cut tree that Larry had bought from the corner market.

It was an event to remember as I handed package after package to my sons, daughter-in-law, and granddaughter. My boys had never known a Christmas like this one. I was enraptured as I absorbed the merriment and surprise in each of their faces. Then, of course, it ended way too soon.

Matthew Morrison had driven his car back to Kansas City to see his mother for the holidays and to pick up some things he wanted for his apartment. So, as they had pre-arranged, Richie piled on a couple more things and hitched a ride back with Matthew to Philly on December 27. As I squeezed Richie tight, I told him I would see him again soon, and then he was off.

As Larry hauled the tree to the local recycle pile, I carefully packed away all the ornaments and garnishings and carried them down to our basement storage closet. I was still basking in the glow of the most incredible Christmas I could ever remember, when, two weeks later I received the following e-mail from Richie:

Subject: Pray for me
Date: Thu, 09 Jan 2003 06:29:56 -0600

Mom,

I need you to pray for me. I've been going through depression since the holidays. I hate my job and I barely make ends meet. I know you are struggling with the same thing. I really want to make something out of myself. I know I am young and if I hang in there I can figure it out. I just don't feel young when I wake up in the morning. I have so much weight on me its hard to breathe sometimes.

On a positive note I've been talking to a girl that lives in Baltimore. She's helped make my days better. We have a lot in common, more in common than anyone I've ever met. We've been talking for a couple of weeks. Her name is Jill.

Well, I'm off work today so I'm going to go into the mall in the city and see if they have any job openings there. I've reposted my resume on careerbuilder and monster.com. I haven't gotten any leads yet though. I would kill to have a real job. I wish I had been more serious about school. Well, I'll talk to you later. Don't worry too much about me, I'm sure this phase will pass. Maybe it's just the bad weather.

I love you,
Rich

I tried to call him but got a machine the remainder of the day, so I e-mailed him the next morning. I asked him to tell me all about Jill. Richie had never had a serious girlfriend, despite his strong desire for one, so I knew that if anything would lift his spirits it would be falling in love for the first time. And it worked.

But just about the time he and Jill progressed past online chat and started making plans to meet in person, Richie's car disappeared. After a lot of panic and confusion, it was determined that the City of Philadelphia had mistaken it as abandoned and towed it away. Richie had overlooked the fact that his Missouri license plates had expired – a fact that was not lost on a conscientious Philadelphia police officer. By the time Richie had located the right party to call, the towing and storage bills had added up to much more money than he could rake up — and more than the car was even worth — so he had to forfeit it.

Not only did this make it impossible to drive from Philly to Baltimore to see Jill, but it was incredibly difficult to get to work. With no extra money to pay bus fares or save for another car, and with his roommates having conflicting schedules, Richie was out in the cold. Literally.

He sent me an e-mail with some of his concerns:

Subject: hi
Date: Sun, 26 Jan 2003 16:55:20 -0600

Mom,

Ok so I'm definitely in love. This situation is killing me. I sent my resume to labor finders. They have an office here. I have to either find a way to get my car back or get another one. Because right now I can't see Jill. And we can hardly deal with it. At this point I will get 2 jobs to get a car, I don't care. I have to make something happen soon. I don't even know if I will stay here after August. There is nothing for me here. Well pray for me. That's all for now, I just wanted you to know how my life is going. I hope you are doing better. I love you.

Rich

By early February 2003, he had swallowed his pride and asked me if he could move back home long enough to buy another vehicle. That way, I and other family members could assist him with rides, and he wouldn't have to pay rent and utilities, so he could save the price of a car more rapidly. Of course I welcomed him back with open arms.

When he first got home, he was determined to find a good-paying technical job. At first things seemed promising, but then all the good leads fell apart. By March he had caved in and filled out an application at the Passantino's Sun Fresh grocery store near our home for a lowly sacker position at $6.00 per hour – the least wage he'd ever earned, other than his first job as a teen at McDonald's.

But things went much better than he expected. He immediately established a good rapport with Dante, the young manager whose family owned the store, then swiftly grew to admire and respect not only Dante, but his family and other managers as well...and they were very good to him. They allowed him a long weekend from time to time to fly out to Baltimore and visit Jill at her parents' home.

On the first such occasion, I received a humorous phone call from Richie. It seems he had gotten the idea that he shouldn't meet his Lady Love with an acne outbreak. So he had doubled or tripled up on the new antibiotic prescription he had just obtained from our doctor.

"Mom, I've known this guy for fifteen minutes, and I stop his toilet up. Then I spend the rest of the day out behind his house puking my guts up!" The circumstances surrounding Richie's initial introduction to Jill's father provided great fodder for future railing from Richie's brothers.

By the end of May, Richie was absolutely convinced that he had found the love of his life. He hinted to me that he and Jill were discussing a future marriage. They had gone so far as to discuss what names they would give to their children some day.

"When you've told someone everything about you, and she says she loves you anyway, that's something." I knew by his words that Jill had made Richie feel it was safe to be transparent with her.

Richie anguished over the fact that he and Jill weren't going to be able to spend much time together that summer while she was on break from her university classes, so I honored his request to invite Jill as our houseguest for the month of June. We would fix up the bedroom in the basement for her, and Richie would fly out to drive Jill back in her car. That way she wouldn't be afoot while she was in Kansas City, and she had a phobia of flying besides.

Richie called in several times from along their route to make sure I had things ready for Jill's arrival. He explained that Jill came from a much more lavish home than ours, and he was afraid she would be uncomfortable if things weren't nice enough. I mused at the new mushy side of him that I had never seen before. I playfully promised I would try hard not to embarrass him.

I will never forget meeting Richie's Jill. It didn't take long to discover why he was drawn to her. She was a small, delicate little girl with long, blond hair, who clearly adored Richie. He once wrote in an e-mail, "She calls me 'Richie.' And I like it." He had trained most other non-family-members to call him 'Rich,' a more grown-up version of his nickname.

Shortly after Jill arrived, Richie surprised me with the news that he had decided to stay in Kansas City long enough to finish up his telecommunications degree at DeVry. So, with Jill at his side, he went and enrolled for the summer trimester, which was to begin in July. Richie appeared energized, with a new determination to get his future mapped out.

July 4th weekend arrived, and Richie and Jill headed back in Jill's car to Baltimore as planned. After a couple of days with her folks, Richie flew back to Kansas City. Unfortunately, he had spent all the money he had made up to that point having fun with Jill, so his car fund was still at zero, which was a frustration for him. Yet he treasured the relationship.

However, Jill wasn't the one that was about to change his life forever…someone else had entered the picture that June.

Chapter 4

The Orchestra Begins

Richie wasn't able to start back at DeVry in July 2003. His W-2 from Saladworks had gotten lost in the mail between Philadelphia and Kansas City, and by the time he had located it, tax returns couldn't be filed in time to complete financial aid paperwork. So his enrollment was put on hold until November when the fall trimester would begin.

His life did get better, however. Jennifer Wright had come home for the summer from Wesleyan College, located in the northeastern Oklahoma town of Bartlesville. She took a job in the deli section of Passantino's Sun Fresh and befriended Richie right away.

Jenn's existence became known one evening when she provided Richie a ride home from work. She had a warm, bubbly, flamboyant individuality that would set her apart in any crowd. Richie's first information shared about her was, "That's Jenn. You'd like her. She's real Christian." Straight to the point, as usual.

But what Richie didn't know is that not long before that evening I had prayed that God would send someone into his life that was a strong believer in Christianity. Since we had lived in Kansas City it seemed that all the people with whom he'd had the closest contact were agnostics or atheists, who had presented many challenges to the beliefs he had embraced as a child. This caused his mind to be filled with doubts and confusion. My specific prayer was, "God, send someone to Richie that will reinforce his faith in Jesus. Send him a Hadley Baker."

Hadley, Richie's older brother, is a youth evangelist…a hilarious one. Hadley's antics are well known throughout many parts of Texas and southern Oklahoma. The kids to whom he ministers always put in a request for him to revisit.

Hadley and Richie adored each other and prized any occasion they had to be together. Hadley could coerce Richie into nitwitted stunts that Richie would never concoct on his own — like dressing in outrageous outfits and going to a Royals baseball game, or backing their car through a fast food drive-up window because…well, just because.

Richie once told his Dad that if he could pick any one person in the world to be like, it would be Hadley. Panged by his own inhibitions, Richie admired Hadley's free-spirited nature.

"Hadley proves to everyone that you can have a lot of fun without doing anything bad," Richie once observed – a point he felt a lot of individuals his age had missed. Unfortunately, Hadley and Richie lived eight hours apart, which limited the time they could share.

Imagine my excitement when Richie made his second statement to me about Jenn — *"She's a lot like Hadley."* I was thrilled, but at that point I had little concept of just how much of an answer to my prayer Jenn really was, nor did I realize how much she would affect Richie's future…but I would soon learn.

As Jenn and Richie grew closer they spent hours in conversation about God and spiritual things. Jenn felt that Richie was searching for God. She wasn't able to answer all the thorny questions he put to her, but she stayed dogmatic in her beliefs. She pointed out to Richie that doing life on his own had left him empty, so maybe he should give God a go.

She would later remark, "For some reason I was in ministry mode from the very beginning with Rich. That's not the way I usually am with people I've just met."

Furthermore, Jenn introduced Richie to her friend Adam, also a student at Wesleyan College and a strong Christian. I felt like I was getting a double answer to my prayer.

One evening I went to pick Richie up from work. Just as we pulled from the parking lot he said, "I've been feeling uncomfortable lately." I thought he was making reference to the effectiveness level of his Zoloft — but he corrected me.

"Jenn tells me I'm under conviction. She said she's been praying for me. I've started reading that *Mere Christianity* book by C.S. Lewis again. It's just so hard to believe." The tone of his voice said, "But I *want* to believe."

I gently explained to him that Christianity is a matter of faith, so most everyone goes through times where it takes some effort to believe. I relayed to him that when I personally go through those times I look at the feast days ordered by God through Moses in Leviticus 23 of the Bible. I detailed for Richie several of the prophetic implications found there and how they have so accurately come to pass...and with his logical brain, he understood the colossal odds stacked against their fulfillment. We talked of the types, symbols, and foreshadows found throughout the entire Old Testament that paint a vivid picture of man's redemption that was ultimately accomplished by Jesus Christ.

Richie became noticeably eased. He said in spite of the issues he had had with God in the past, he wanted me to know that he desired and planned for his children to be taught the same things he had been taught.

During the night of August 3, 2003, Richie and I had horrifying dreams, which left us both shaken. Richie had dreamed his Dad had died; I had dreamed that Brandi Cummings had only been given a month to live.

Brandi was the 26-year-old daughter of one of my closest friends from middle school, Carla. Brandi and Richie had played together as children. Brandi had been fighting cancer for close to a year. Following surgery, chemotherapy, and radiation, however, the doctors were hopeful they had eradicated it from her body.

Richie began trying to phone his Dad, and I began trying to call Carla. Richie was never able to get an answer, but I did. It was almost as if I already knew when I heard the news – the cancer was back; the doctors had declared there was nothing further they could do. They were sending Brandi home to be cared for by Hospice for however long she had left. I was numb as I hung up the phone numb.

When Richie found out that my dream had in essence come true, he became panicky and began trying to reach his Dad with greater fervor. He e-mailed his sister, Aja, at Oklahoma State University, who told him that Mike and Jackie had been out of town. Richie relayed his dream to Aja. He asked her to tell him more about their Dad. He had an urgency to know his father in a deeper way.

On August 29, 2003, Brandi Cummings died. She hadn't even lasted a full month. Richie was convinced he was about to lose Mike Patterson. A couple of days later, as we were headed to Richie's work, he said woefully, "I wish I could have gotten to know my Dad better."

"Well, Richie, just try calling him again."

The permeating sadness in his answer unveiled the desperation he felt. "I've been trying, but I can't reach anyone."

Richie didn't have many dreams, and the ones he did have he was exceedingly moved by. Just a few weeks earlier, as he had slept one night, he had seen an entrancing little blond-haired, blue-eyed boy. The following morning he was radiant as he described the child.

"I can't wait until I have kids," he raved. "Maybe he is going to be one of my sons."

The boy's face was so imprinted in Richie's mind that Richie felt he would recognize him if ever he saw him again. Richie had been the spitting image of the way he described the child when he himself was a young boy. I determined that someday if Richie had a son I would ask him about the dream again and see if his son looked familiar to him.

About the time Brandi died, Richie, Jenn, Adam, and some other friends had just returned from a float trip. Richie had had a wonderful time, but immediately following the trip Jenn and Adam had returned to college. Going to work in the produce section, to which Richie had since been promoted, was suddenly not nearly as enjoyable. The deli and produce departments were side by side, so Jenn's absence was painfully noticeable.

As Richie climbed into the car the first day after Jenn was gone, I asked him my usual question, how his day had gone.

"Terrible," he said. "I miss Jenn."

It was a three-hour drive to Wesleyan College in Bartlesville, Oklahoma, and Jenn's old red Dodge Omni wasn't up to many trips home, so Richie's desire for his own wheels escalated rapidly.

A young man who Richie had met at the store had a small, black Toyota for sale. It was pretty rough, but it ran and had good tires; it just needed a battery. And amazingly the price was only $250. Richie emptied his car fund, and the young man drove it over and parked it in front of our house.

Another weekly paycheck would be necessary in order for Richie to buy the needed battery and insure and license the car in his name. So it set idly to the side of our driveway as he eagerly awaited payday.

On September 10, the Wednesday following payday, Richie spent the first of two days off work getting his car drivable and legal. He had his sister-in-law, Tiffany, take him to get his Missouri drivers license renewed and to purchase a battery, spark plugs, and other miscellaneous items for the car; and Larry helped him change its oil.

At around 3:00 P.M. that day, Richie called me at work to 3-way me in with an insurance rep to do a direct phone check using money he had given me to hold for him in my account – money he had wanted to get out of his own possession so he wouldn't be tempted to spend it. The insurance policy would be in effect at midnight that same night.

At 11:30 the following morning, September 11, I picked Richie up from home during my lunch break. From the drive-through at the McDonald's near our house, we headed to the Jackson County Courthouse in downtown Independence, Missouri. Richie took care of his property tax and obtained the required receipt. As I returned to work, Richie got in his little black Toyota Celica and headed out, with glee, to complete the licensing process.

His first stop was at an inspection station, then he drove to the Department of Motor Vehicles at Hwy 291 and 23rd Street in Independence to get the title transferred and acquire his plates. The waiting line at the DMV was long, so approximately 45 minutes later Richie finally got to see an agent, who pointed out to him that the young man who had sold him the car had not signed the title. The bill of sale was insufficient.

Richie was almost beside himself as he headed west on 23rd Street. His mind was buzzing as he tried to figure out what to do. He didn't have any idea where to find the seller at that moment, and he was anxious to complete the process of tagging the car, so he decided he would just sign the title himself. He reasoned that it wouldn't hurt anything, since he was obviously not stealing the car.

He pulled into a Bank of America on his right and used a pen from one of the tellers. Needing to make a left turn to head back east on 23rd Street to return to the DMV, he pulled from the bank lot across the two inner, westbound lanes. Paralleling himself within the continuous center turn lane of 23rd Street, he navigated forward, and glancing back over his right shoulder and seeing that the eastbound lanes were clear for him to enter, he pressed the accelerator.

As he rotated his head back around he looked right into the eyes of John Jenkins, the driver of a small O'Toole Automotive delivery truck that had shot out in front of Richie past a stop sign from a side street. With no time to react, Richie plowed into the end of John Jenkins's left front bumper.

There were no apparent injuries to either driver, so, after the police came and filled out a routine accident report, Richie drove the car home.

I answered the phone at my desk and listened as he told me he had just had a car wreck, banging up the entire front of his car. His mood was that of disbelief. "My car is totaled, and it barely even damaged the other guy's pickup."

He described what had happened and said the officer had told him he would have to study the situation and decide whether either driver should receive a ticket. If so, the officer would mail it to them.

The officer had told Richie that since he had come from a parking lot into 23rd Street and John Jenkins was entering 23rd Street from a "regular side street," it might be Richie's fault. Richie was puzzled by this because, in Richie's words, he "was parallel with 23rd Street and the other guy was perpendicular to 23rd Street" when they collided. Richie didn't see how it could be his fault since he knew he was "there first." He said he would have T-boned John Jenkins if John had been just a little farther into the street. As it was, Richie had only clipped him.

I tried to comfort and calm Richie by assuring him that it sounded like he had established the right of way before John Jenkins entered the roadway. I told him not to worry about it, that at worst it might be a no-fault type wreck – he would just have to file an insurance claim and see what happened. After agreeing to talk more about it that evening, we hung up.

At around 8:30 P.M. that night, Larry and I returned home from a weekly Christian Motorcyclists Association dinner ride. Richie asked me if I would cut his hair, something I had done many times throughout his life. Since it was Thursday, a work night, I normally would have asked him to wait until the following night. But since Richie had had a rough day and I wanted to spend some time with him, I agreed.

He asked if I might be able to do something a little different with his hair this time, maybe a little more trendy. Richie's hair had been curly and blond when he was small. As he had grown into an adult it had become a wiry, wavy brown muff. I always joked with him that his hair never got long, it just got fat.

We decided to re-create a look he'd had a couple of years previous when a barber had cut his hair in a particular style and then lightened the color of it. He thought coloring his hair might even be a hoot for Jenn, who liked to do outlandish things herself.

But since he was still a bit nervous about his mother's hair color on his head, I eased his fears by offering to do a couple of test strands on some of the long ends of his hair that would be cut off. He agreed, and I applied the test color. We then waited for approximately 50 minutes for the color to process. During this time Richie went back and forth a couple of times to his downstairs quarters to exchange instant messages with Jill and a couple of other friends. He also made himself something to eat in the kitchen, chatting with me while doing so.

Among other topics, he brought up the fact that his Uncle Darrell's father, Dalton Blundell, had died that day after being adjoined to our family the 22 years Darrell had been married to my sister Cheryl. Richie noted that Dalton's death had occurred on the date 9/11 and that his niece Olivia was born on 9/11 the previous year, making this day her 1st birthday. He wondered aloud that 9/11 looked "like it might turn out to be a monumental date for our family."

Finally it was time to wash the hair color from Richie's test strands and check the results. After a trip to the upstairs hall bathroom mirror, he decided to go ahead with the color. So I told him I would first cut his hair and then apply the color. I spent approximately one hour cutting his hair, as it was very difficult to cut where it would lay nicely. During this time we were stationed in the living room and the TV was on. Richie and I laughed from time to time at the silly movie that was on, but we were mostly visiting about the events of Richie's day and most especially about his wreck.

Richie's mood was light. He had gotten over the initial shock of losing his car and had even expressed to me that "the wreck might actually turn out to be a blessing in disguise." Because, after thinking about it, he was sure it was the other guy's fault. And maybe the insurance company would total Richie's car and give him more money than he'd paid for it, and he'd be able to buy a better car. "I'm not sure the other one would have made it to Bartlesville to see Jenn and Adam, anyway," he mused.

"See," I said, "every time you think it's the end of the world, God turns things around and you end up with something better."

Several years before, Richie had lost a job from RPS after being there only a few days, because a superior of the man who had hired him realized he wasn't yet seventeen years old. Company policy mandated that all employees be a minimum age of seventeen. At that time Richie had called me pouting that he had "lost his good-paying job." To which I had replied that he should pray about it, that God would work it out. Sure enough, by the next day he had gotten a better position with better pay at UPS.

Richie's only negative statement to me about his wreck the remainder of the evening was that he knew he had gotten "a hard jolt" and would "probably be feeling it tomorrow."

It occurred to him that the next day was his payday. Since he was scheduled to work from noon to 8:00 P.M. the next day, he asked me if he could take me to work the following morning and keep my car. He wanted to pick up his check from Sun Fresh and run some errands before his noon start time. I agreed. He added that this would allow his co-workers to get "their laughs" about his new hair-do over with ahead of his work shift.

Throughout the course of cutting his hair I stopped several times to check out a strange swelling of Richie's head around both of his ears. I knew this was something I had never observed before, but I didn't get particularly worried about it because Richie's behavior and conversation were completely devoid of abnormalcy, and he wasn't complaining of discomfort. I finally dismissed it as maybe having something to do with a scalp condition Richie had had for years. This would turn out to be a costly mistake.

I applied the hair color to Richie's entire head, but I had trouble getting it in close around his ears because the usual gap between Richie's ears and head was greatly reduced by the swelling. I did the best I could without getting the color formula on any bare skin.

When I washed the color from Richie's head I immediately saw there was a problem. In trying to avoid getting the dye on the skin of Richie's ears, I had failed to get the hair directly around and behind his ears saturated with color. He had reddish blond hair everywhere on his head except for thin dark rings around each of his ears. I assessed out loud to

Richie that this would not work – it made him look ridiculous. So I mixed up another small amount of the hair color and re-applied it to the problem areas. This time I pulled his ears away from his head in order to get better access to the hair around them.

After the required time had elapsed, I washed his hair once more, and this time everything looked fine. We expressed to each other how tired we were and bade each other goodnight. It was 12:20 A.M. Richie headed downstairs, and I headed to bed. When Richie got to his quarters, he noticed Adam was online so he exchanged a couple of instant messages with him. Adam happened to be on the phone with Jenn at the time, so Richie and Jenn exchanged hellos vicariously through Adam. Richie then told them he was exhausted and going to bed. They all exchanged goodnights and talk-to-you-tomorrows.

The next morning, Friday, September 12, 2003, sometime between 7:30 and 8:00 A.M., I went down and awakened Richie, asking him if he still wanted to get up and take me to work and keep my car to run errands that morning. He sleepily said he'd just get his paycheck when he got into work and forget the rest of it for that day. I reminded him I was going to a monthly luncheon with some former co-workers, pointing out that he'd have to call Tiffany for a ride. He said OK, set his alarm for 9:40 A.M., turned over, and snuggled up in the covers to go back to sleep. I left for work. The world was good…or so I thought.

Chapter 5

A Smoldering Wick

It was wonderful to see my DST friends at lunch that day. The food was good and the conversation better. The small group at the table was made up of employees of the company for whom I had originally moved to Kansas City; one of the nation's largest processors of mutual funds trades. Roger, who had been my partner during my tenure there, gave me advice as to what fund he felt I should invest in for Olivia's future. Her first birthday party was going to be that evening, and I wasn't satisfied that I had yet found her precisely the right gift.

A little before 4:00 that afternoon I finally found a chance to take a break from my work and call the number that Roger had given me at lunch. I began to inquire of the representative that answered the phone about the process for establishing an account with his company for Olivia.

At about that same time, Larry was finishing his workday as an outside parts salesman for a large trucking firm in the Kansas City area. As he headed toward home, he decided to stop in and see an old classmate from East High School. But something prompted Larry to keep driving when he reached his friend's place of business — he needed to go home first.

When Larry first reached our house, he used the hall bathroom. While he was there he noticed hair collected on the shower drain.

Richie forgot to clean up after himself, Larry thought. *I'll have to remind him.* When Richie had first come to live with us, we had established as one of the house rules that Richie would always clean the shower after he used it. And it was rare that he would fail to do this.

Larry moved on to the kitchen and fixed himself a soft drink. He then went to the basement to start a load of clothes in the laundry. When he opened the lid of the washing machine, he saw that there were already clothes there that needed to be dried. As he tossed them into the dryer, he recognized them as Richie's work clothes. The Sun Fresh uniforms were unmistakable.

Just about then Larry heard a loud snoring sound coming from the other side of the basement. He thought to himself that it was awfully late in the day for Richie to still be sleeping. Richie must be taking a nap. Larry mused to himself that Jill had been justified when she had teased Richie about being a loud snorer during the time that she had stayed in our home.

Larry reloaded the washer and proceeded up the stairs to leave the house and head back to see his friend. As he entered the kitchen, he was quickened by a ringing phone. He almost ignored it, but for some reason he decided to answer. It was Passantino's Sun Fresh. Richie was supposed to have been at work at noon but had never shown.

Larry held the cordless phone to his ear as he descended the steps to the basement and entered Richie's room. He called Richie's name but got no response. After shaking Richie's arm, he still got no response. He told the person on the line he would have Richie phone them back as soon as he could get him awake.

Larry hung up the phone and shook Richie more violently, rolling him onto his side, then back. Still no response. Larry felt unsure about the situation. He knew that Richie was a deep sleeper, but he was beginning to decide something was wrong. He reached again for the phone and called me at work. Hearing my voice mail recording, he depressed the button and continued trying to rouse Richie. A minute later he dialed my work number once more. This time I put the mutual funds representative on hold. Olivia would not get an account that day.

****

When the ambulance left our house that afternoon with Richie, I retrieved my purse from the kitchen table, and Larry and I headed to Independence General Hospital. Along the way we stopped in at Passantino's Sun Fresh. I went in to find Dante. I knew that it would be some time before the hospital would allow us in to see Richie, and I wanted to let Dante know that Richie would not be at work that day nor probably anytime again soon.

"Whoever called saved Richie's life," I declared to Dante. I was exceedingly grateful that the caller had picked that precise moment to ring Larry.

When Larry and I reached the hospital, Larry Richard, who had made it back to Kansas City, and Johnna greeted us. They led us to the private waiting area that had been established for our family by the staff of Independence General. Tiffany and Olivia joined us shortly thereafter; Quentin was away at Army National Guard Basic Training at Fort Benning, Georgia.

After what seemed like an eternity, Dr. Richard Whitney entered the room to brief the family on Richie's status. When I saw his nametag, I quipped, "Your name is Richard, too. It must be a good sign." My mood was crushed when I noticed his grim response to my attempt at light-heartedness.

"I wish I had better news for you," he began. He went on to lay out a bleak picture. The CT scan of Richie's brain was the worst Dr. Whitney had ever personally observed. Richie's brain was so swollen it had crimped shut the vessels leading up into it from the base of the skull. Dr. Whitney explained that both of Richie's internal carotid arteries contained blood clots.

I felt like I had been sucker punched. Until that moment I had been convinced that Larry had been divinely placed at the scene at exactly the right moment to rescue Richie. *This has to be a mistake*, I thought. *God is still going to come through and fix this situation.* After all, why else would God have orchestrated Larry finding Richie just in the nick of time?

My eyes met Larry Richard's, and we exchanged a long gaze that silently communicated to each other our mutual disbelief and feelings of despair. This just couldn't be happening.

Larry asked if clot buster drugs could be used to dissolve the clots in Richie's brain. Dr. Whitney replied that he was in consultation with a neurosurgeon, but that the neurosurgeon didn't feel there were any promising remedies for Richie's condition.

Dr. Whitney told me that he would allow me, as Richie's mother, to come back into the treatment area to see Richie. He was giving Richie no hope for survival.

As I approached the gurney where Richie was lying, my first observation was that his color was perfect. He was nice and warm again. And pink. He looked as though he were in a deeply restful sleep. The presence of the respirator gave the only clue otherwise.

After allowing me some time alone with Richie, Dr. Whitney called me aside and presented to me some medication bottles that had accompanied Richie into the Emergency Room. They had been found in Richie's bathroom by the police officers who had worked the scene, Dr. Whitney explained. Dr. Whitney wanted my thoughts about the bottles. I was surprised to see medications of my own in the collection, including Vicodin and Ultracet; pain medications left over from past episodes of surgery and injury — medications that had for years resided in the cabinet of my private bathroom. Knowing that Richie had never before bothered any of my medicine, of which he was fully aware, and seeing that the medications he was in possession of were for pain, I drew the conclusion that whatever had occurred with Richie, he had at some point gotten into a great deal of pain.

I knew that Dr. Whitney was somewhat concerned that there was another explanation, however, when he questioned me about whether Richie had been depressed lately. Given the old dates that the bottles bore on their labels and the small amount of pills missing from the bottles, Dr. Whitney wasn't able to immediately discern how many, if any, of the pills Richie had taken. But blood and urine screenings returned *positive* readings for acetaminophen, opiates, hydrocodone, PCP, and alcohol. No *levels* were done for any drugs other than acetaminophen. Blood tests revealed that Richie's acetaminophen level was 110, which was quite high. Acetaminophen is sold as the brand name Tylenol and is also a substantial ingredient in various prescription painkillers.

The opiates were in the form of meperidine, which I recognized as the generic name for Demerol, one tablet of which had also been in my private medicine cabinet. But my Demerol bottle was not among the bottles Dr. Whitney was showing me. (I would later discover that the policeman who had rounded up the bottles from Richie's bathroom had merely missed it.)

Dr. Whitney explained that PCP is a street drug. I told him that I had no idea how Richie would have come into possession of PCP, because he never went anywhere except to work, and it was usually me who took him there. I was certain that we had never stopped off along the way to pick up illicit drugs.

I was equally puzzled by the finding of alcohol in his blood. Richie had confessed to me once that he had tried drinking a couple of times, but had gotten deathly sick from it. I had told him that he was his mother's son in that respect, because I had had the same experience with alcohol when I was young and wanting to impress my friends. But, laying that fact aside, I have a strong sensitivity to the smell of alcohol — I detest it. And yet I had given Richie mouth-to-mouth resuscitation without picking up the faintest scent of alcohol. The only alcohol that was present in our home was a bottle of gin I had bought earlier that summer to use in Dr. Atkins' Luscious Lamb recipe. And I would later find that it appeared to still be full, other than the two tablespoons that I had used.

The whole situation was confusing. I knew that Dr. Whitney was trying to investigate the notion that Richie might be an overdose case. And, while I could see why he might feel that way, my knowledge of Richie told me that if Richie had decided to do himself in he would have 1) left a "goodbye and I'm sorry" note for me, and 2) turned the bottles up and swallowed a substantial amount of the drugs. And since Richie had never been an illicit drug user, it wasn't plausible that he had just overdone it this one time as is common in accidental overdoses. I had never once seen Richie under the influence of any kind of substance, so I was mystified as I began trying to sort out in my mind exactly what had transpired with my son.

There were only two possibilities the way I saw it. Richie had either taken drugs to *help* himself or to *harm* himself. Either Richie had gotten into severe pain, or Richie had tried to commit suicide. If Richie had gotten into severe pain, that would explain the presence of the pain medicines in his blood but would not explain the presence of PCP and alcohol. But if Richie had wanted to commit suicide, why were there still so many pills in the bottles? And why had he left untouched my tranquilizers and sleeping pills left over from the days of my clinical depression the prior year? Richie would have known that these drugs would have been a better choice if one wanted to quietly check out. Nothing made sense. I felt totally bewildered.

Even though Dr. Whitney had in essence already pronounced a death sentence over Richie, I asked Dr. Whitney if he could please keep Richie stabilized until I could get my family in from out of state. I needed their support, and I needed time to process what was happening. Dr. Whitney obliged and admitted Richie to the Intensive Care Unit, but he warned me that it was just a matter of time, that they couldn't keep Richie sustained indefinitely. Eventually Richie's cardiovascular system would shut down.

By now it was late Friday evening. I had begun leaving messages with individuals who I thought might be able to help me locate Richie's Dad and Jackie. Eventually a close friend of the Pattersons, who had found one of my messages, called the hospital. He relayed to me that Mike and Jackie were in Las Vegas at a business conference. But he knew their contact number and had already left them an urgent message to call him.

As soon as Richie was settled into ICU, the nurses allowed the family back to spend time with him. Larry Richard and I agreed that we would split that first night into two shifts. I would go home around midnight and return at approximately 3:00 A.M. to relieve him. This would allow us both to get some sleep.

When I got home I made and received several phone calls. Then, just as I was finally dozing off into a troubled sleep sometime after 1:00 A.M., Mike Patterson called from his hotel in Las Vegas. He had gotten his friend's message and called the hospital; Larry Richard had filled him in on details about Richie, as well as informing him that I had gone home for a while.

It felt strange to be talking to Mike about Richie dying. Mike and I had never communicated when Richie was born. I was suddenly aware of how much had changed in 23 years, and I was grateful to God that Richie had gotten a chance to know his Dad. I didn't know much to tell Mike, other than to recap what he had already heard from Larry Richard and to fill him in on what had been going through my mind since this ordeal had begun.

When I returned to the hospital to relieve Larry Richard at 3:00 A.M., Richie's room was frigidly cold. When I had left him, Richie had been covered with a blanket. Now he was only loosely covered with a sheet and had a large fan blowing at high speed directly on him. His nurse informed me that Richie's temperature had soared, and they were trying to cool him down. With my medical knowledge I was immediately suspicious that there was infection somewhere in Richie's body — which might lend an explanation to the fact that his white blood count had been 22,600 at the time he was admitted to the Emergency Room. This additional information only served to further muddy the waters as to what could possibly be the cause for Richie's grave condition.

As the sun came up that Saturday morning, I began questioning the nursing personnel as to when I might expect to see Dr. Leroy Wagner, the doctor on call that had been assigned as Richie's primary care physician. Typically, Monday through Friday doctors make their rounds early before they begin seeing patients in their office — but this was Saturday, so it was anyone's guess as to when Dr. Wagner would appear.

At 7:00 A.M. a pretty lady named Maggie took over as Richie's nurse. She informed me that Richie was being treated solely as an overdose patient. I expressed to her the urgency I felt for a conversation with Dr. Wagner. She assured me that she would see to it that Dr. Wagner knew of my desire as soon as he arrived at the Intensive Care Unit. I stayed at Richie's bedside most of that morning, exiting only to the waiting area to make brief phone calls or visit with friends who had come to check on Richie's condition.

While in his room I expressed several times to various hospital personnel, "I think he's hurt." But they always seemed to discount that the wreck Richie had been in had anything to do with his condition.

"He would have marks on the outside of his body if that were true," was one example of their disclaimers.

By late morning I had still not seen any sign of Dr. Wagner, so I once again voiced my concerns to Maggie that I would like to talk to Richie's doctor. This was met by a look of surprise on Maggie's face. She explained that Dr. Wagner had been there earlier and that she had communicated to him my desperate desire to speak with him. She had let him know that I was in the ICU waiting room anytime I was not at Richie's side. She apologized for his having failed to make contact with me and asked if I would like for her to page Dr. Wagner. "Yes, I would. Absolutely," I said.

It was clear that Richie's condition was not improving, so I looked up the number for the American Red Cross in order to acquire their help in bringing Quentin home from Fort Benning to be at his brother's side. However, I did not want to get tied up on the phone for fear that Dr. Wagner would answer the page and I wouldn't be available to take his call, so I delayed calling them.

After quite some time had passed, Maggie very meekly apologized once again for Dr. Wagner's behavior and told me she had just paged him the second time. But once again there was no response from Dr. Wagner.

I believe that Maggie had just paged Dr. Wagner for the third time when the phone at the ICU Nurse's Station finally rang. Maggie allowed me to take Dr. Wagner's call there.

"Dr. Wagner, I'm sorry to bother you, but I've been very anxious to talk to you about Richie to see what the game plan is for his care," I began.

"Well, the game plan is we're going to try to stabilize his blood pressure and keep his heart and lungs working and see if this thing reverses itself," he growled.

I was taken aback by the lack of any expression of sympathy on the part of Dr. Wagner, as well as the gruffness of his voice. But without making reference to his poor manners, I continued. "See if *what* turns around? What do you think is wrong with Richie?"

Dr. Wagner's tone betrayed his impatience with me. "Well, it's obvious your son has taken an overdose of Tylenol to commit suicide." My head started to spin at his words. *Suicide*? OK, maybe. But from *Tylenol*?

"This doesn't make any sense. If Richie was trying to kill himself he wouldn't have bothered with Tylenol. He had much stronger drugs at his disposal," I reasoned aloud.

"Ma'am, Tylenol is the drug of choice in many suicides," Dr. Wagner retorted.

"But, Richie wasn't suicidal. He's had a history of depression, but he's been fine lately. I have spent a lot of time with him. I know." I was trying to give Dr. Wagner a picture of my son, but he remained unshaken in his opinion of what had happened to Richie. "If you talk to the survivors of most suicide victims they will tell you that the person was extremely happy right before they did it. Because once they've made the decision to do it, the pressure is off of them."

"But they don't buy a new toothbrush and other personal care items if they've made that decision," I argued. Richie had purchased these things only two days before we had found him down.

Dr. Wagner did not relent in his effort to convince me that there was no explanation for the shape my son was in other than that it was self-inflicted.

Finally, in exasperation, I burst out, "So, what are you saying, that he took 20 or 30 Tylenols?"

"It would have been more like 40 or 50," came Dr. Wagner's reply. My heart sank. Dr. Wagner was a professional, right? And if he could tell by Richie's blood acetaminophen level that Richie had apparently swallowed 40 or 50 Tylenols, then there was little more I could say. I had no further defense against a man that for some unknown reason was seemingly delighted to prove me wrong. I wilted as I hung up the phone.

How could I possibly tell my 74-year-old mother that the grandson in whom she had invested so much of her life had killed himself and hadn't even bothered to leave a note to say goodbye to her or me or anyone else that he loved so dearly? I was physically ill. Richie had apparently not only taken the small amount of prescription pain pills we had found missing from my medication bottles in his bathroom but had emptied the Tylenol bottle that was still in my cabinet as well.

I went to the phone and called the Red Cross and asked them if they could get word to Quentin's unit that Quentin's brother was currently on life support not expected to live. They required a precise medical diagnosis, so I told them that Richie had evidently attempted suicide by drug overdose. After they spoke to Maggie and verified the diagnosis, they assured me the message would be sent within the hour.

Larry Richard had meanwhile picked up Hadley and his fiancée, Christie, from the Kansas City International airport at around 1:00 P.M. I returned to my family and tried to put on a brave face for all members present until I could figure out the words to use to tell them what I had just learned.

It was past lunchtime, so we all decided to retire to Larry Richard's house to eat and relax for a few minutes. LaRetha and her husband, Billy, arrived with my mother by car at approximately 3:00 P.M. to join us there.

As we were about to leave to return to the hospital I asked my family to gather in the den. My voice was weak as I relayed to them the conversation that I'd had with Dr. Wagner earlier that afternoon. When I finished speaking, I looked over to see that the color had drained from my mother's face. She seemed to have gone somewhere far away within herself. The room was quiet. Everyone sat in stunned silence for several minutes. We finally composed ourselves and very soberly headed back to Richie's bedside.

That afternoon Larry went to Jenn's grandmother's house, right around the corner from our own house, to get a message to Jenn at college. Jenn and Adam arrived at the hospital together sometime between 4:00 and 5:00 P.M. They were heartbroken to see Richie's condition.

As a family we all talked to Richie, having faith that he could hear us somewhere in his spirit. We exhorted him to find a way to make things right with God. Believing he had committed suicide, we all had great fear for the welfare of his soul. My heart broke as I watched each one lean over Richie and gently kiss his forehead as they spoke tender words of comfort and love to him. How could he have chosen to leave these people that he was so crazy about?

"Richie, find Jesus and ask Him for help," I begged. "If you can't find Jesus, find Grandpa and he will help you find Jesus."

Richie's Grandpa, my Daddy, had died June 27, 1992. Daddy was a devout Christian and had been a wonderful spiritual leader for our family until the time of his passing.

Jenn and Adam, as well as Hadley, stayed late into the evening with Richie, reading the Bible aloud, praying with him, and singing Christian songs. Hadley and I left around 11:00 P.M. to try and get some much-needed sleep. By that time, only LaRetha, Larry Richard, Jenn, and Adam remained. When I returned to the hospital at 6:00 A.M. Sunday morning, I found Hadley alone with Richie. Hadley explained that he had relieved Larry Richard at 3:00 A.M. and that the others had been gone since shortly after midnight.

As I walked into Richie's room, my first observation was that he was sporadically jerking in what might be described as strong shivers. I questioned Hadley as to how long this had been occurring, as up until that moment in his illness I had never seen Richie make the slightest move. Hadley informed me that at sometime around midnight, Adam, alone with Richie at the time, had come running out to the waiting room to inform the others that Richie had begun drawing his hands toward his face. Hadley said that Richie had continued that throughout the remainder of the night, but shortly before I arrived he had converted to doing nothing more than the shivering.

Hadley left to go and rest, and shortly thereafter LaRetha arrived at the hospital. At 7:00 A.M. she and I were required to leave Richie's room for the hour-long nursing personnel shift change.

At 8:00 A.M. LaRetha and I attempted to return to Richie's room, but we were turned back by the nurses, who informed us that they were setting up to do an EEG on Richie. They wanted to measure his brain activity.

As we waited, Pastor Brian Ross dropped by on his way to Sunday morning services at Englewood Assembly of God Church, where Larry and I, Richie, and Quentin's family all attended. I excitedly told Pastor Brian that Richie had begun moving and that I felt maybe he was turning the corner.

Pastor Brian assured me that he would have the church pray diligently that morning for Richie's recovery, and he left.

I was anxious to see what Richie's EEG would show, expecting to get some good news. LaRetha expressed to me that she felt Richie was "coming back to us."

Suddenly we heard a voice call out over the hospital's speaker system. "Code Blue, ICU! Code Blue, ICU!"

"Uh, oh," I said to LaRetha, "someone's in trouble."

After watching several hospital personnel go rushing by to enter the double doors leading into the ICU, LaRetha calmly arose from her seat and walked over to where she could look through the glass windows into the ICU corridor.

She instantly turned and bolted toward me with a look of unspeakable horror in her face, as she blurted out, "Oh, it's Richie! Let's pray!"

We collapsed into each other's arms, and oblivious to the other visitors in the waiting room, we began to weep aloud and pray that God would intervene for Richie. A sinking, suffocating agony, which defies description, was sweeping over me.

The day that we had found Richie, even as horrible as it had been, he had still been breathing, and I had immediately called 9-1-1 and then started performing CPR on him until the medics had arrived. I had felt somewhat comforted by the fact that he had just needed some help and I had gotten that for him. And surely that had provided a sort of guarantee that everything would turn out OK. . . hadn't it?

But now it was different. He had *had* help. There was nothing more that could be done. And it just wasn't enough. Period.

I felt like I was drowning – I couldn't draw a breath. I buried my face in my 5-foot, 9-inch sister's chest and groaned from the depths of my soul. "Hold him, God," I wept, "hold him." I didn't know why I was saying those particular words, it just seemed to be all that would come out.

I was aware of LaRetha crying hysterically. "I stand in the gap for him, Lord, I stand in the gap for him," she was demanding.

Then, the most amazing thing happened, for which I still have no explanation. It was as if someone had taken a huge invisible paintbrush, and with one stroke had painted an immediate sense of deep calm simultaneously over the two of us. We both, at precisely the same second, became completely quiet.

I pulled back from LaRetha enough to look up into her face, five inches above my own. Through the tears that were streaking her face, there was an almost unearthly glow about her.

I began, "Did you feel that…," and with a luminous smile she finished my question, "…that peace?"

"Yeah," I whispered.

"I don't know what just happened, but we have won in the spirit. I'm not sure about physically, but spiritually we've won. Richie is OK," LaRetha declared. I could feel the truth in her words.

Just about that time I had the most overwhelming sensation that my Dad was somewhere close by and that he had come to get Richie.

The chaplain came out and told us that they were doing everything they could to save Richie but that it was looking bad.

Minutes hung like hours until a nurse finally emerged and escorted me back to see Richie. She explained to me that they had an IV adrenaline drip flowing, fully open, into Richie's veins in order to keep his heart beating.

She asked me to what lengths I wanted them to go in order to keep him with us. I told her I would be grateful if they could keep him in a "life-like" state until Quentin could get there. I didn't want him to see his brother for the first time as a corpse, and I felt that it wouldn't be that much longer before Quentin would be arriving.

The nurses concurred with my wishes and cut into Richie's femoral arteries so they could begin pushing large volumes of IV fluids into his body to keep his blood pressure from bottoming out.

Shortly afterwards, all the members of my family currently in town congregated back at the hospital. Jenn and Adam returned, as well. We all took turns at Richie's bedside.

At one point, while LaRetha, Hadley and Larry Richard were sitting with Richie, a man they described as "fat and sloppily dressed" came into the room and stood at the foot of Richie's bed, asking them about taking Richie's organs for transplant. My son and siblings were appalled by his lack of sensitivity. The man turned out to be Leroy Wagner, Richie's doctor who had been so rude to me on the telephone.

I was furious when I found out that Leroy Wagner had talked about organ transplantation while standing in Richie's presence. During my nurse's training years before, I had been taught that you always, always, always assume that the patient can hear regardless of how the situation appears.

Because Richie had declined being an organ donor on his driver's license, plus the fact that my mother was unable to handle the thought of it, I respectfully denied the request for them to remove Richie's organs.

A few hours later my remaining sibling, Cheryl, and her husband, Darrell, arrived from Texas with their children, Lindsey and Rusty. They had buried Darrell's father, Dalton Blundell, the day before and had left Texas that morning to make the 8-hour journey to Kansas City.

That evening I got a call from Quentin. He was not going to be arriving in Kansas City until the following morning.

I talked to Jackie Patterson, who informed me that Richie's Dad would be flying to Kansas City the next morning also.

Unfortunately, in spite of tremendous efforts to keep him in this present world, Richie's heart stopped and he was pronounced dead at 10:25 P.M. that night, Sunday, September 14, 2003. A ghastly silence fell over the room as the rhythmic hissing of the respirator ceased.

Other than Quentin, every member of what Richie had called "the family" was present. Pastor Brian Ross was there to lead us in prayer. Then we each took our turn saying goodbye to Richie.

Larry Richard had fallen to his knees in anguish as he held onto the railing along the side of Richie's bed to steady himself. This sight caused my heart to break even further.

Pastor Brian walked with me down the long hallway out of the ICU. Numb with disbelief, I asked Pastor Brian if he thought it was possible that Richie could have still gone to heaven even if he had committed suicide. Pastor Brian responded that he thought it was possible. He felt that Richie's spirit had lingered near his body until the moment his heart had stopped and that he could have still prayed to God during that time. This brought me great comfort.

The other thing that continued to bring me comfort was the refrain I was still hearing in my head from the song I had heard on the bridge: "Remember He is in control." I didn't understand, but somewhere in the farthest recesses of my mind, I felt that God must know why all of this was happening. And, somehow, right now, that was enough to keep me going.

I requested that an autopsy be done, and the Jackson County (Missouri) Medical Examiner's office was called to retrieve Richie's body.

Pastor Brian drove me home.

Chapter 6

A Prophecy Is Given

Two weeks after I had attended Brandi Cummings's funeral, I was planning a funeral for Richie. I made arrangements with a funeral home to fly Richie's body to Will Rogers Airport in Oklahoma City following the autopsy. The funeral home would then receive it and transport it to their facilities in Duncan, Oklahoma, approximately eight miles north of Comanche.

Comanche was where I had been raised, where my mother still lives in the family home, and where Richie and I had both spent our lives until our move to Kansas City when he was fifteen years of age. I wanted to take Richie back to Comanche to bury him next to my father.

Jackie Patterson contacted the pastor of Ray of Hope Church, where Jackie and Mike and their children attended. It was the same church in which Brandi's funeral had been held, and it was only a couple of miles from Comanche's Fairlawn Cemetery, where Brandi and my father both rested. Richie's funeral and burial were scheduled for 10:00 A.M. Thursday, September 18, 2003.

Billy and LaRetha took my mother and left on Monday, the morning following Richie's death, to go back to Comanche. Mom was having a difficult time mentally and emotionally, and LaRetha felt it would be better for Mom to be back in her own surroundings. LaRetha also agreed to my request to assist Jackie and Mike in choosing the gravesite, casket, and clothing in which Richie would be buried — tasks I didn't feel I could bear.

Hadley and Christie also left on Monday, flying back to Dallas so that Hadley could arrange and record a song that had dropped into his heart about Richie. He wanted to have it ready in time for Richie's funeral, and he didn't feel that he would be able to perform it live without breaking down.

I wanted a memorial service to be held in Kansas City so that our many friends here could be with us to lend us strength in our time of loss. Pastor Brian agreed to host the memorial at our local church at 10:00 A.M. Wednesday, September 17, 2003, the day preceding the funeral in Oklahoma.

Planning the order of the services was not difficult. Despite the fact that I had never dreamed I would be preparing the memorial and funeral of one of my children, I immediately moved forward with great clarity about my choice of scriptures and songs. I requested that both pastors work John 11:25-26, Isaiah 42:3, and the entirety of Psalm 27 into their eulogies of Richie.

I arranged for the CDs of Ray Boltz's *The Anchor Holds,* Larnelle Harris's *Were It Not For Grace,* and Karen Wheaton's *I Know A Love* to be played. And, of course, the most beautiful song of all would be Hadley's tribute *Brother of Mine.*

Larry Richard put together a beautiful computerized slide show of Richie's life set to the Joe Cocker song *You Are So Beautiful To Me*, to be shown at the end of each of the services.

I asked Shirley Doyle, a concert pianist currently living in Washington D.C., to whom I had been close since we had met in first grade at Comanche Elementary, to play *The Lord's Prayer* at Richie's funeral.

Wednesday, September 17, 2003, Pastor Brian helped me welcome many friends, including current and former co-workers of Larry's and mine, as they assembled in the Englewood Assembly of God church to help celebrate the memory of my son. RJ Lansing and other of Richie's friends, along with their families, were there, as well, to say goodbye. And I was touched to see Frank Passantino and a group of Sun Fresh employees in attendance. Several members of the Christian Motorcyclists Association, of which my husband was serving as president, came to offer their support.

Pastor Brian did a spellbinding job painting a picture of who Richie was. Even though Pastor Brian didn't know Richie personally, it was almost as if he had a sixth sense about him.

As Pastor Brian read Isaiah 42:3, "A bruised reed He will not break, and a dimly burning wick He will not extinguish…," (NASB) I knew I had selected this passage for a reason. Even Pastor Brian realized that Richie was "a bruised reed," and pointed it out to those who had gathered there.

In addition to the scriptures I had requested, Pastor Brian read parts of the eleventh chapter of Hebrews. My heart melted as I heard him liken Richie's condition to those described in Hebrews 11:14-16.

"Richie counted himself a stranger and a pilgrim in this earth, and he sought a better country," Pastor Brian opined.

How could there ever be a better description of Richie? I thought to myself. *And how could Brian Ross, with his limited knowledge of Richie, have so perfectly nailed it?*

As Pastor Brian read the entirety of the twenty-seventh Psalm, as I had requested, it dawned on me that a lot of it didn't really seem to fit Richie, and there was very little of it that was even comforting. But, for some reason, I had felt compelled to have the whole thing read, and it still seemed right.

At the conclusion of Pastor Brian's message, he asked the audience to bow their heads. He explained that he was going to say a prayer for them. But before he prayed, he inquired of them as to whether anyone present would like to establish a personal relationship with Jesus Christ. He instructed anyone who wanted to do so to quietly raise their hand, and in doing so they would be saying, "Yes, Pastor Brian, the prayer you are praying is for me." Pastor Brian would tell me later that five hands went up that day. I knew that with Richie's shy condition he would have had trouble ever winning that many hearts to Christ in his lifetime, so I was thrilled.

Immediately following the memorial Larry and I, as well as Quentin, Larry Richard, Cheryl, and their families, got into our cars and sped toward Duncan, Oklahoma, where we would attend Richie's visitation that evening.

Just a few miles outside of Kansas City I reached for Larry's cell phone and dialed the number of the Jackson County Medical Examiner's office. I wanted to speak to Tom Hinsley, the coroner's investigator that had been assigned to Richie's case, and Tom only worked at the ME's office Sundays and Wednesdays.

I hadn't spoken to Tom since he had phoned me just before midnight Sunday night after I had arrived home following Richie's death. I had told Tom at that time that I couldn't come up with any reason why Richie would have killed himself. "Unless the wreck upset him a whole lot more than any of us realized, I just can't imagine why he would have done this," I had explained, and then I had suggested that Tom might call Jill and see if she had any information to offer.

However, since Sunday night I had become suspicious that the suicide theory just wasn't adding up. By now Larry had filled me in about seeing signs that Richie had taken a shower and started his laundry the day we had found him —

his usual workday routine. Richie was a typical college kid. He loathed doing laundry. He wasn't going to do laundry until his cleanest dirty shirt smelled too bad to wear. If he had decided to leave this world, the last thing he would have worried about was his laundry.

I had also found a list of "things to do" on Richie's bedside stand, tasks that Richie had been feverishly attending to on the two days he had been off work just prior to that fateful Friday. The list detailed a plan for life, not death. For example, putting together a financial budget and wrapping up loose ends for his upcoming trimester at DeVry University were among the items that appeared on the list.

And at the bottom of the page Richie had made a note, "Get these things done by October." Knowing himself to be the procrastinator that he was, he had set himself a deadline.

When Tom Hinsley answered the phone I went into a full dissertation about why I felt he needed to look past suicide for the cause of Richie's death.

"He may have taken too much medication, Tom, but Richie had no sense about medication dosages," I concluded. "I don't believe he was intending to hurt himself. I'm thinking he was in pain."

I detailed to Tom the event that had occurred the first time Richie had gone to visit Jill's family in Baltimore, when Richie had made himself ill by taking too much of his antibiotic.

As I was finishing the story, Tom interrupted me. "I think you need to talk to Dr. Gale," he offered. "He's the doctor that did your son's autopsy. He's right here if you'd like to speak to him."

"Wow, that would be great," I replied.

I immediately felt a rapport with Dr. Thomas Gale. He was warm, chatty, and forthcoming.

"Dr. Gale, I've been so anxious to learn what you've been able to discover about the cause of Richie's death. You know the doctor at Independence General has ruled him a suicide." My earnest plea was met with a chuckle.

"Well, the one thing I can rule out for sure is suicide." His words were like soothing water flowing over my aching heart.

"If you had been in the room with me when I performed your son's autopsy, you would have heard me say to my colleagues, 'I know this kid has a rough looking toxicology report, but I think he just had a heck of a headache and perhaps overdid it a bit on his Tylenol trying to get some relief'," he continued.

Being the detailed person that I am, I informed Dr. Gale that I was a nurse and exhorted him, "Talk to me."

And talk he did. He explained to me in great detail that two days earlier he had checked my son's remains and had found that Richie had died from trauma. Everything he had found was consistent with whiplash injury, to be exact. Richie's brain showed the same markers as those found in shaken baby syndrome.

Furthermore, Dr. Gale gave me more than one good reason as to why Richie's death couldn't possibly be drug related. "You're fortunate that your son lingered for a couple of days, giving any medications he had taken time to work through his system. If he had taken enough drugs to have hurt him, his liver would have telltale signs. I have checked the liver microscopically, and it is perfectly clear. Drugs had absolutely nothing to do with your son's death. Besides, the timeline doesn't work for suicide."

He debunked the hospital's findings of phencyclidine and alcohol in Richie's blood as well. Dr. Gale had used a more accurate form of testing, using the hospital's first-draw blood, which showed the earlier results had been false positives.

After approximately 45 minutes of a fruitful exchange of information, Dr. Gale informed me that he would have all required legal paperwork finished in about two weeks, and we ended our conversation.

I was ecstatic to call ahead to my family in Oklahoma and give them the news. Richie hadn't committed suicide! Likewise, I put in calls to the Pattersons and my pastor. I wanted to shout it from the rooftops.

When I finally arrived at the funeral home that evening, a sizable crowd had gathered. I was apprehensive about entering the room where Richie's body was on display. No experience in my past had prepared me to see one of my children lying in a coffin, and I wasn't sure I wanted to do it for the first time with an audience...but there didn't seem to be much choice.

Fortunately LaRetha had been there to see to the details of making him look as natural as possible. She had re-arranged his hair, as the funeral home had combed it in a style much different than Richie's usual.

Mike and Jackie and their children were standing beside Richie, receiving guests, as I accessed the inner chamber where he rested. The presence of the Pattersons helped to put me at ease.

I looked down into Richie's face and was struck by how old he looked. He had become swollen and bloated during his final hours of life as the hospital personnel had pumped massive amounts of IV fluids into his body. Now all of that fullness was gone, and his skin had draped back into position with many new creases having appeared.

After many hugs and quiet conversation with loved ones, the family left the funeral home.

The following morning I awakened to a gray and hazy sky. "This is a perfect day for Richie's funeral," I declared to everyone present. "He always liked overcast and rainy days." This was an oddity that Richie and I had shared. I have been told that persons who suffer from anxiety difficulties often prefer cloudy days to bright ones. Intense light tends to over-stimulate the senses and worsen the condition.

Unfortunately, as the morning wore on the sun appeared. By the time 10:00 A.M. arrived, it was a radiant day.

The funeral home sent private cars to my mother's home, as well as the Pattersons', to drive the families to the Ray of Hope church. As my family entered the foyer of the beautiful structure, Mike and Jackie and their children were just ahead of us. They led the family procession into the sanctuary where many friends and some of Richie's former teachers had gathered. I was keenly aware of how honored Richie would be that his father was leading his mother's family in a public display of mutual love for Richie. I asked Jenn and Adam to walk next to me as we made our way to the front of the church. When we were seated, Larry was at my right and Jenn was to my left.

If a funeral can be beautiful, Richie's was. Following the playing of *The Anchor Holds*, the assistant pastor of Ray of Hope and a longtime friend, Dow Pannell, began the service by reading the obituary and offering his encouragement to the family. Hadley then eulogized his brother, recounting many funny stories from their youth, followed by the playing of *Brother of Mine*. His song was poignant and touching. I was shocked that he could have composed something so resplendent in such a short amount of time.

Pastor Mike McCord then delivered the funeral sermon. Having buried a young son of his own in the recent past, Pastor Mike was especially sensitive to our feelings. Following my instructions, he began his comments by thanking Jackie on my behalf for being such a wonderful example of Christ's love to Richie. "You didn't just passively tolerate him, but you reached out to him with the gentleness and tenderness of a mother," Pastor Mike read from my note. "You took him into your home and allowed him the opportunity to experience being part of a nuclear family, which meant the world to him." I wanted Jackie, as well as the world, to know the feelings of gratitude and respect that I have always maintained towards her, and never more than on that day.

As Pastor Mike read the entirety of the twenty-seventh Psalm, I once again was struck by how little of it seemed to pertain to Richie, but it still felt right that Pastor Mike was reading it.

Pastor Mike then eloquently described the hope that we have that we will see our children again. "The resurrection is not a *day*," Pastor Mike proclaimed, "it is a *Person* — it is *Jesus*."

"And we know what God has saved our children *to*, but we have no idea as to what He might have even saved them *from*," he continued. I felt in my spirit that Pastor Mike was making an accurate point; I wasn't sure what would have been in Richie's future here on earth, but I was sure that his future was now bright.

Pastor Mike closed by introducing Shirley at the piano. She didn't miss a note as her fingers danced across the keys, sending *The Lord's Prayer* resonating through the large expanse overhead. When she struck the last note the crowd was in awe.

Once again the slide show of Richie's life was shown, and once again it brought tears of both joy and sorrow to all eyes watching.

Next, the church was quiet for a brief time as the funeral directors opened the lid of Richie's casket in preparation for the procession of those who wished to view Richie's body as they said one last goodbye.

As the first mourners began to make their way to file past the coffin, Shirley began to play quietly on the piano. She began high in the treble keys with a tinkling, childlike rendition of the old church anthem *Jesus Loves Me*. Other than *The Lord's Prayer*, I had not made any specific requests as to what songs Shirley would play, but her choice had touched at least one heart very deeply. Jenn laid her head onto my left shoulder and gasped, "Oh, that's what I sang for him that night in the hospital!" As amazing as that was, it would pale in comparison with what would come a little later.

I was the last to approach Richie's coffin. I had watched as each member of the family had taken their turn. My heart had almost seized as I had seen Larry Richard come close to collapsing as he had staggered from his seat toward Richie's body.

Now it was my turn to look into the face of the dearest on earth to me for one final time. As I stood there I could vividly remember the very first time I had looked into that face. I remembered the little creases that had appeared at the inside corners of his upper eyelids, one of the first things I had ever noticed about him. Knowing that once I turned and walked away and this moment ended I would never see him again in this life, I lingered. I touched his face and stroked his hair as I had done so many times before. I wanted to capture every detail in my mind so that it would never disappear from my memory.

It was bittersweet to see the neatly cropped haircut that I had given him on that last night that he and I had spent together. I couldn't help but smile at the reddish blond color that he had been sure would give Jenn a hoot. Then I laid my head on his chest and told him how much I loved him and how sorry I was that life hadn't been better for him. I asked him to forgive me for my part in that.

Eventually Hadley became worried about me and came to see if I was all right. As he slipped his arm about my waist, I motioned to Shirley to come to my side as well. I didn't want her to keep playing and miss the chance to say her goodbyes. She left the piano and joined me. As we stood holding each other, the church was once again quiet for a few moments.

Then, the most unusual thing happened. The church's sound engineer, a young man that I didn't know personally, started a CD on the sound system to fill the air. He couldn't have known how his selection would affect me. I caught my breath as I heard the sounds of *Sweet Hour of Prayer* filtering through the sanctuary. *Sweet Hour of Prayer* is an old hymn that I have always associated with my Daddy. It is not a song that I have ever heard many times in church, but one that Daddy used to sing while he was busy taking care of his farm animals or doing chores around the house as I was growing up. Having been in charge of the music at his funeral, I had insisted on having that song sung by the best singer I could find in that area. Now, without any planning on my part, it was being played at Richie's funeral. The feeling I had experienced at the hospital that Sunday morning during the Code Blue episode came rushing back. Was Daddy indeed somehow letting me know that Richie was with him? I wondered.

As the white hearse left the church to head to the cemetery, a line of traffic followed. When the procession entered the drive at Fairlawn, the vehicles scattered and came to rest on the graveled lanes that formed a grid among the graves. The pallbearers — three of Richie's brothers; his cousin Rusty; a childhood friend, Brian Wilson; and a former Royal Ranger leader and mentor, Rodger Smith — were the first to emerge. They carried Richie's casket to a waiting platform that had been constructed just above the gravesite. A temporary canopy served as a roof under which the family would be seated for the interment ceremony.

As family members and friends exited their automobiles, a sudden and bizarre rain shower erupted, which sent many scattering back to their cars to retrieve umbrellas, while others hurriedly took refuge under the canopy. The bizarreness of this came in light of the fact that the sky for miles in every direction was sunny and bright, so much so that most of the people were wearing sunglasses.

"This is so strange," I heard one lady say. "That rain must be coming in on the breeze from a long way off."

Strange, indeed, I thought. Richie had gotten his rainy day after all.

As soon as the crowd had moved into place, the rain stopped just as suddenly, and the brief graveside service began. We committed Richie's body back to the earth from which it came, and his soul back to the God from Whom it came.

The family was then transported back to Ray of Hope for a noon meal that the church had provided.

When it came time to return to my mother's house, Larry and I realized that we had gotten too involved in conversation and that all family vehicles had left the church without us. Hadley and Christie had done the same. We were all stranded and had to ask Shirley for a ride. Why was I not surprised when Shirley explained that her rental car was a mid-size? She had requested a compact car, but when she had arrived at the rental car company they had been fresh out of compacts and had given her a mid-size for the price of the compact. Larry, Hadley, Christie and I had a comfortable ride back to Mom's house. But our rest would be short-lived.

Chapter 7

27:12

I returned home to Kansas City the weekend following Richie's funeral. On Sunday night I received a call from my mother-in-law, who had a message for me. A friend of hers wanted me to contact her son, Tim, who is an attorney in Kansas City. His mother knew I would need help with the legal matters surrounding the wreck, and Tim handled such cases.

So the next morning, Monday, September 22, I phoned Tim's office and arranged to meet him in his downtown high-rise the following day.

By the time I met Tim I had learned, through some research, that he was known for having a highly respected, ethical law practice. This was important to me. I didn't want some 'ambulance-chasing' lawyer that would make a spectacle of the situation.

I took Tim a copy of the accident report filed by the police and asked him to review it and determine whose fault the wreck had been. I further asked that if the wreck was deemed to be the fault of the O'Toole driver that Tim handle getting O'Toole's insurance company to pay Richie's medical, funeral, and burial bills — which were astronomical.

I informed Tim that Leroy Wagner had tagged Richie as a suicide, but that an autopsy had been performed and I had already spoken to Dr. Gale at the Medical Examiner's office, who had advised me that the wreck was the express cause of Richie's death.

Tim agreed to look into the accident and to administer the settlement of any financial issues that arose. I left, feeling confident I was in good hands.

After two weeks had passed, I placed a call to Dr. Gale to see if the autopsy paperwork was complete, as he had predicted it would be. He told me he was still waiting on the final histology reports, so it would probably be a few more days. I thanked him and told him I would check back.

Just before hanging up, I conveyed to Dr. Gale my deep gratitude for his having taken the time to explain to me the details of Richie's autopsy on the day I was traveling to Oklahoma for Richie's visitation.

"You'll never know what it meant to me and my family to be able to bury Richie knowing the truth of what killed him," I proclaimed. "Thank you so much for telling me it wasn't suicide, that it was just the wreck."

"Well, I can't really say for sure it was the wreck," Dr. Gale stammered hesitantly.

"Oh, really? What was it then?" My mind was instantly whirling. I caught my breath as I anticipated Dr. Gale's presentation of new evidence that he had uncovered. I knew he would be more than ready to fill me in.

It didn't take more than a few seconds, however, to realize that Dr. Gale's demeanor had changed since our prior conversation. When I had talked to him two weeks earlier, he had been open, unshielded, even friendly. Now he was guarded and seemingly measuring his words. He sounded as though it was a discomfort for him to talk to me. I found this quite troubling.

"Well, it's hard to say, but I think if it was the wreck he would have known immediately he was hurt," he muttered. "And it seems he would have had a seatbelt mark on his outer body."

I felt perplexed by the fact that this doctor had gone from apparently knowing all the answers to suddenly not being sure of anything.

"Dr. Gale, I have heard of many people who have been injured in wrecks that didn't know it immediately. And I've also known people who were in some pretty hard collisions, even some with chest injuries, where there were no outer marks from seatbelts on their bodies. Is there some other reason you now doubt Richie died from whiplash trauma, or is this it? I mean, have you gotten some new lab results in or something?" I questioned.

He confirmed that he had no evidence other than what he had cited in our first conversation.

"Well, don't you remember making the statement to me that if I had been in the room when you were doing Richie's autopsy that I would have heard you say to your colleagues that Richie would have had a heck of a headache? What about that?" I continued.

"That was just my first impression," he said weakly.

"Then what has happened to change your impression?" I demanded.

"Well, it's just hard to say what the cause of death was," he replied.

"What do you mean? Didn't you tell me everything you had found was consistent with whiplash trauma?" I countered.

"Well, yes, but it's just hard to say that's what killed him," he responded.

"Then what killed him?" I was starting to feel shaken. "Dr. Gale, do you remember about the strange swelling I told you I had seen around Richie's ears the night before we found him down? What do you think that meant? I'm sure it had something to do with what happened to him. The only reason I didn't make more of it at the time is because Richie was acting so normal and not complaining, and I finally convinced myself maybe it had to do with his chronic acne condition."

"What doctor treated him for acne? Is it possible for me to get those records?" he inquired.

"You think *acne* killed him?!" I exclaimed.

"Well, it's just hard to say," he repeated again.

I hung up the phone in total astonishment. *What just happened?* I cradled my face in my palms as I shook my head. I felt totally rattled.

I immediately placed a call to my attorney. "Tim, I may have been premature in asking you to handle Richie's wreck; I just now talked to the coroner again, and he's telling me he's not sure anymore that the wreck is what caused Richie's death." I must have sounded dazed as I gave Tim the details of the conversation I had just had.

"What is the doctor's name you spoke to?" Tim asked.

"Dr. Gale," I answered.

"Oh. I know this guy; he's got some problems." Tim advised me to try to stay calm and just wait until Dr. Gale published his ultimate report. "We'll see what he says, and if we need to, we can get an independent autopsy," he concluded.

For the next three weeks I checked each Monday to see if the autopsy paperwork was ready for pickup. On each occasion I was informed that it was not.

I then received a call from Tim's office. He wanted to see me. I nervously waited in Tim's lobby for several minutes before he came out and invited me into his private office. His words would pierce my heart.

"I'm afraid you don't have a case here that you can win," he voiced. He had just received Richie's hospital records from Independence General, and Leroy Wagner had done a number on Richie's reputation. Leroy had Richie listed as a "probable," not "possible," mind you, but a "probable" suicide. Richie's records were filled with notes about a drug overdose and alcohol poisoning, as well as his being poisoned by about every other substance known to man — even the Lidocaine the ambulance personnel had given him. But the most exasperating item in the records was a statement by Leroy Wagner on Richie's History and Physical form: "Patient presently unmarried. No stable family relationships." Just when I had thought I couldn't possibly be more upset. Once again, I was shaking.

How dare he? I steamed. *This man has never even met our family. He doesn't have a clue who Richie even was and never thought Richie was worth his time! Now he's writing this kind of trash on Richie's permanent, legal documents!*

The appall I felt only got worse when I realized that the first 'believer' of this hurtful nonsense was my own attorney. He was, in essence, showing me the door. He didn't wish to handle Richie's affairs any longer.

"So, you're telling me that if a young man is out here driving down the road, and someone runs out in front of him and he's injured, then just because he gets into his mother's medicine cabinet for some pain medicine due to the fact his brain is swelling out of his head as he's dying, that excuses all liability from the person that caused the wreck?" I was incredulous.

"No, I'm not saying that it excuses all liability, but you've got to understand I have to pick and choose my cases, and I don't think your case is one I can afford to spend time on," he explained.

"Well, I do feel like it's worth spending time on, so I guess I need to ask you if you can recommend another attorney who might be willing to help me," I responded.

"You might try a guy we lovingly refer to as 'Wild Bill'", he said. "He's known to take on some cases that are real flyers."

About that time I remembered the name of another attorney that had helped an acquaintance of mine a few months before, so I asked Tim if he might be able to talk to him for me instead. Tim told me he would put in a call to the guy on my behalf, and that I should call him myself the following day to set up an appointment.

That night, as I was lying in bed, I kept hearing the name 'Wild Bill' echoing in my head. Each time it would pop into my mind, I would dismiss it. But it never seemed to stay absent from my thinking for long.

The next morning I put in a call to John, the new lawyer, and sure enough, Tim had given him notice that I would be contacting him. John was somewhat abrupt with me and told me to give him a call back when I got the autopsy results and the death certificate in hand. I knew instantly that this was not someone I wanted to deal with. I immediately phoned Tim's office and asked his assistant if she could give me the full name and contact information for the lawyer that Tim said was known in the legal profession as 'Wild Bill.' "Oh, that would be Bill McIntosh," she revealed. She then gave me his number. I was stunned to realize that, other than the prefix, his number was the same as my work number: 6464. I experienced a settled feeling that I had found the right man for the job.

I called Bill's office and told his receptionist that Tim had mentioned Bill's name to me, and I needed some help. She did a quick screening of the facts and told me Bill would call me if he was interested in taking the case. I knew he would be…I knew that he was supposed to be my attorney. I was right.

When I met Bill I immediately liked him. He was an earthy fellow with a calm demeanor — very approachable and easy to talk to. I signed paperwork to transfer the case to him.

A week or so later, on Monday, the 27th of October, I made my usual weekly call to the coroner's office. This time their answer was different. I was told by the young lady who had answered the phone that the Patterson autopsy was finally finished.

"Good," I replied. "It's 12:00, so I'll just run down there on my lunch break and pick it up from you."

"Well, it's done, but it hasn't actually been signed by the doctor yet," she explained. "That won't be done until this afternoon."

"I see. Well, maybe I can come by right after work, then. How late do you stay open?" I asked.

I didn't hear her answer, because something she had just interjected into the conversation had taken my breath away. "They are going to rule him a suicide," she had gleefully declared.

"*What?*" I gasped. "A *suicide*? Based on *what*?"

"They found a thing he had written on livejournal.com a few days before he died, where he was real depressed." She was almost crowing, like they had found a prize.

"I know about that. He wrote that one night when he was bummed out over his childhood friend dying, but that wasn't something he would kill himself over. He hadn't been in touch with Brandi for years. Besides, that was only that night," I explained. "He was fine right after that." I then impatiently demanded to speak to the person in charge.

"That would be Dr. Yager, the chief Medical Examiner," she declared.

"Give me his phone number, please," I requested.

I hung up the phone and rang the number she had given me. A man answered and I asked to speak to Dr. Yager. As the man was explaining that Dr. Yager wasn't available, that

I would have to leave a voice mail, I recognized Dr. Gale's voice.

"Dr. Gale, is that you?" I snipped.

"Yes," he replied.

I plowed into him. "I want to know what's going on down there. You told me weeks ago that the one thing you could rule out for sure with Richie was suicide. Were you mistaken? Were you confused? *What?* "

"Well, we have to give our best opinion, and that's our opinion. You just don't want to accept it." The condescension in his voice made me bristle.

"Accept it based on *what*?" I fired back. "Give me a reason to accept it. You don't have blood counts that indicate overdose. You told me the liver was clear. There weren't enough pills gone from those bottles to kill someone. So what are you basing this on?"

He had nothing else to offer, so I insisted that he put me into Dr. Yager's voice mail. I asked Dr. Yager to call me immediately, that I had an issue I needed to address with him. I was livid.

My blood pressure must have risen to a dangerous level, because suddenly I couldn't breathe. The lights in the room were too bright….and the air was stifling. I grabbed my purse and bounded down the back stairwell through the door leading outside. I jumped into my car and within a couple of minutes I realized I was driving round and round the block surrounding my building. My mind was spinning. *What am I going to do? This is crazy! I know…I'll go down there. I'll make Dr. Gale look me in the eyes and tell me why he's doing this!* I pointed my car toward the coroner's office.

When I arrived I walked into a humble waiting room containing a small glass window. I rang the buzzer, and when the attendant, Ashley, stepped to the window, I asked to see Dr. Gale.

"Just a moment," Ashley replied. She then took about three steps around a corner, getting just beyond my line of vision, but certainly not out of my hearing, and I listened to her tell Dr. Gale I was there.

"Well, what does she want? I just talked to her. Tell her I'm not here," I heard him blurt.

Ashley stepped back in front of me and, with a straight face, announced, "He's not in right now."

"I just heard you talking to him." I made no effort to hide my annoyance.

Turning slightly red at being called on her lie, Ashley stepped out of sight again, and this time there was only quietness coming from the other side of the wall. When she re-appeared she announced that Dr. Gale was "on his way out for his walk."

"How long will he be walking?" I seethed.

"He's usually gone about an hour and a half," came the reply.

"I'll wait!" I defiantly plopped down on the bench just outside the window.

After approximately ten minutes had gone by, a door opened and Dr. Thomas Yager stepped out and invited me back into the hallway that led to his office. *He must have come in since I left the message for him,* I thought to myself. *That's good; now we'll get to the bottom of this, and he'll do something about Dr. Gale's behavior!* I couldn't have been more wrong.

I tried to remain calm and keep my voice even as I laid out for Dr. Yager what had transpired within the past six weeks. I tried to be specific and detailed when I related to him all the things that had been said to me by his deputy Medical Examiner.

For an hour and a half I cried, begged and tried to reason with Jackson County's chief forensic officer. To no avail.

"Don't you know how *cruel* this is?" I pleaded. "To Richie? To me? To my family?"

He was unmoved. His eyes were emitting a blank, glassy stare as though his mind was somewhere else.

He flippantly fanned through the pages of Richie's autopsy report and callously stated that he didn't see anything like what I was describing contained in it. He went so far as to say there was nothing found in Richie's body that would be associated with trauma.

"Dr. Yager, I don't care what that report says, I know what Dr. Gale told me on the 17th of September," I argued.

"Dr. Gale is an excellent neuropathologist, and if he says it's suicide, then it's suicide," he pronounced.

"But you don't have scientific evidence to back that up," I pointed out.

"Well, what would you like for me to rule it?" he asked coldly.

"If you can't figure it out, then just rule it 'Undetermined'," I suggested.

I'll never forget watching Dr. Yager roll his eyes. "I can't do that," he retaliated. "I'm bound by law to examine all the evidence and give my most accurate opinion as to what happened, and my opinion is that your son killed himself. You're just not willing to accept it."

This was like a bad dream I couldn't wake from. About that time, Dr. Yager looked past me to the hallway, where he had just seen Dr. Gale walk by. "I think you need to talk to Dr. Gale about this." His tone was not such that I felt he wanted Dr. Gale to help me….it was more like he was anxious to pass me off to someone else and be done with me.

For another hour and a half, I repeated my pleas to Dr. Gale. Thomas Gale would never look me in the eyes. Every time I would pin him on an issue, he would revert back to, "Well, this is just my opinion, and you won't accept it."

Exasperated, I finally placed pictures of Richie's mangled car in front of him, and leaning toward him, I asked, "Dr. Gale, are you telling me that the day after this kid has taken a hard jolt in a wreck, there's *no way* he would have *any* pain of *any* kind *anywhere* in his body that might compel him to take pain medicine?"

"No," he said insolently, as he tossed the pictures back at me. "Now, the wreck might have caused him *emotional* pain; maybe that's what drove him over the edge," he surmised.

I collapsed back into my chair. For whatever reason, this man was determined to write *suicide* on Richie's death certificate. I felt helpless and destroyed.

"Well, this is obviously going nowhere, so I'm going to leave now," I stated. I weakly gathered my things and headed toward the door.

"Yes, and we have given you quite a great deal of our time," he taunted me with one last cruel jab.

I numbly walked back to the street where I had left my car next to a coin meter, which had long since expired. Tucked under my left windshield wiper was a parking ticket issued by the city of Kansas City, Missouri. I thought I would explode as I kicked the front left tire of my car.

When I got back to my office, I expected my boss to be looking for me. I figured I was in trouble, seeing how I had taken quite an extended lunch hour without garnering permission from her first. But, remarkably, when I went and offered explanation she hadn't even missed me.

I sat down at my desk. I could feel my heart pounding in my head and chest. Every muscle in my body seemed to be quivering, and I felt short of breath. *You've got to calm down*, I kept repeating over and over to myself, *you're going to have a stroke*.

I looked over at my side table and saw my Bible laying there, open to the 27th Psalm. It had been that way since I had returned to work from Richie's funeral, but I hadn't really looked at it in those six weeks. *Maybe reading the 27ᵗʰ Psalm will calm me down.*

As my mind was replaying the ugly scene at the coroner's office, my mouth was mechanically reading the words of King David, written thousands of years before. Suddenly, I stopped. Verse 12 had just jumped off the page at me. "Deliver me not over unto the will of mine enemies: for *false witnesses are risen up against me, and such as breathe out cruelty,*" it said (KJV, emphasis mine). I swallowed hard and read it again. Just as I had finished reading it the third time, the thought hit me, *Well, it never fit Richie before, but it sure does now!* On the 27ᵗʰ day of the month at the 12ᵗʰ hour, Psalm 27 verse 12 had become like a fulfilled prophecy. Now I knew why Psalm 27 had had to be read at Richie's services. God was letting me know that what had just happened was not a surprise to Him. Right away it got a little easier to breathe.

I realized I didn't have the required concentration to finish my workday, however, so I dialed 'Wild Bill''s number. *If another lawyer is going to quit on me, then I might as well know it right now; I can just go on home and shoot myself,* I thought. Not really. But that's how distraught I felt.

Bill told me to come on over, he was immediately available to see me. Little did I know at the time what a miracle that was in itself.

When Bill saw me the first words out of his mouth were, "Man, you don't look too good."

"I'm *not* too good," I assured him.

"Well, sit down and tell me about it."

There are no words to describe the comfort that Bill's demeanor brought to me in that moment. I felt as comfortable as if I were talking to my own father. In the natural scheme of things, there was no reason for anyone who didn't know Richie to believe he hadn't killed himself. The hospital had said so, and now the Medical Examiner was saying so. But, astonishingly, Bill didn't abandon me....or Richie. I don't even remember much of what Bill said; I just became acutely aware that he was with me. And that I, indeed, had the right lawyer. For the first time that day, someone was listening to me, and it gave me the courage to fight — courage that I would desperately need.

I would immediately begin re-exhibiting symptoms of the clinical depression I had suffered in 2002, with sleepless nights and raging nausea, necessitating calls to my mother before dawn, when I would be hanging over the toilet bowl, to have her pray me through episode after episode.

On the way home from Bill's office that evening, I came to the conclusion that I would have to sue the coroner in order to clean up Richie's death certificate. *But, if I sue the coroner, the news media will be all over it,* I cringed. I quickly had visions of reporters being at my door, and I recoiled. But, then I felt a strong rebuke in my spirit. "Don't you *dare* back away from this," I heard a 'voice' saying in my head. "This is so much bigger than you and Richie; I'm going to answer someone else's prayer who has been hurt by this coroner's office. They don't know how to fight this battle, how to find the truth, but you do. I've given you the personality, the knowledge, and the background to make you perfect for the job. *You can do this.*"

The message was clear. My reply was short: OK.

Three evenings later I went to see the psychiatrist who had taken care of me in 2002 and literally saved my life. I poured my heart out to him and told him of the anxiety I was dealing with. He put me back on medication, something that I struggled with but was willing to do, because I knew if I got back into the shape I had been in before I would not be able to handle the task at hand.

On the way home I stopped to fuel up my car. As I stood in the chilly October air watching the dial spin on the pump, I offered a forlorn prayer to heaven. "God, there is someone out there who can tell me what happened to Richie. Please help me find them." Immediately the name "Mark Doherty" popped into my head, and I once again heard the voice. "Call Mark; he'll know what to do."

I rushed home and dialed the dentist in Pryor, Oklahoma, who had many years before married a close friend of mine. I hadn't talked to Mark in ages. When he answered I told him my dilemma and asked for advice. Mark is one of the smartest, most analytical people I have ever met.

"Don't you have a medical school there in Kansas City?" he probed.

"Yes, KU Med is right on the other side of the city from me," I replied.

"Here's what you should do….go over there in the morning and find the pathology department. Tell them you want to speak to the most brilliant person they have on staff. Give that person this case and let them tackle it. Those guys love to solve mysteries, and they are proud of being able to be the one who figures out the truth in a situation. And since they're in a different state, there won't be any conflict of interest, so it's perfect." His suggestion was something I would have never thought of on my own.

The following morning, Halloween day, 2003, I telephoned the pathology department at Kansas University Medical Center in Kansas City, KS. "I need to speak to the brightest, most brilliant pathologist there," I stated, just as Mark had instructed me.

"You need to speak to Dr. Kathy Newell," came the reply from the friendly voice at the other end of the line. "She's actually a *neuro*pathologist," he explained.

"Even better," I affirmed.

I left a voice mail for Dr. Newell, which she returned a few minutes later.

I began trying to present a hypothetical situation to her. I thought maybe I could get information from her without prejudicing her opinion with too many facts of Richie's case.

"Dr. Newell, can you tell me how long it would take for clots to form in someone's brain after they quit breathing effectively?" I conjured.

Dr. Newell seemed to find the vagueness of my question difficult to address.

After a couple of exchanges, Dr. Newell finally pressed me to the point. "I assume we're talking about someone you love."

A dam broke inside me, and the tears started to flow. "Yes, it's my son. Please help me," I blubbered.

"Why don't you just start at the beginning and tell me what happened," she coaxed.

I began with Richie's wreck and went through the swelling around the ears all the way to the CT scan readings in the ER, at which point Dr. Newell stopped me. She seemed to zero in on Dr. Whitney's ER diagnosis: Bilateral Thromboses of the Midline Cerebral Arteries. "Are you certain that was his diagnosis? Because *bilateral* thromboses would be extremely rare," she contested.

After assuring her that Richie's ER record indeed listed bilateral thromboses, and after filling her in on the car wreck as well as the finding of pain medicines in his system, Dr. Newell requested that I fax her a copy of Richie's ER record, the Toxicology report from the hospital, and the CT scan interpretation. She also desired to see the autopsy report, but I hadn't yet received a copy from the coroner's office, as it was still awaiting a signature on the day I had been there, and I hadn't yet regained enough strength to make another trek down there.

Dr. Newell told me that she would look over the documents, but it might be a day or two before she could get back to me, as she was very busy. I told her that would be fine, I was just grateful for her help.

Fifteen minutes after I had faxed the paperwork, however, my phone rang. "This is so wrong," Dr. Newell fumed. "I'm a mother, too, and I want to help you."

Dr. Newell explained that bilateral thromboses of the midline cerebral arteries would not, could not, ever be caused by drug overdose. She informed me that she had worked in the past for the Poison Control Center, so she was qualified to say that an acetaminophen level of 110 is a *therapeutic* level. Furthermore, she added, she couldn't understand why the ICU doctor and Medical Examiner had both ignored Richie's history of a motor vehicle accident within the previous 24 hours of his admission to the hospital.

After we hung up Dr. Newell took it upon herself to pore over the medical literature and retrieve several articles relating minor motor vehicle accidents with cerebral clots and death within 24 to 48 hours following the event. She made copies and mailed them to me at her own expense. I, of course, provided duplicates to Bill.

Meanwhile, I went back to the Medical Examiner's office and obtained copies of both the Autopsy Report and the Investigative Summary regarding Richie's case, which I faxed to Dr. Newell.

After further review Dr. Newell approached me with a very delicate subject. She wondered how I would feel about having Richie's body exhumed so that she could take a look inside his head. I didn't hesitate to grant her wish. I told her I would speak to Bill and get it arranged.

But first, I wanted to present to Dr. Yager the research that Dr. Newell had produced. I rang the ME's office and stated to the young lady who answered the phone that I would like to make an appointment for my husband and me to see Dr. Yager. She made note of my name and immediately put me on hold.

After a few seconds she came back on the line and asked me which case this was pertaining to. It didn't seem to be so much a question as verification that it was the Patterson case. She then put me on hold again.

After a bit, a male voice came on the line and snapped, "May I help you?" Somewhat startled, I re-stated that I was trying to set an appointment with Dr. Yager. "You've already talked to him," came the berating response.

"Yes, you're right, I have, but at the time I talked to him I hadn't gotten an actual copy of the autopsy report. Now that I have a copy, there are some issues I'd like to discuss with him." I struggled to remain polite.

"Well, do you have anything new?" he retorted.

"Yes, as a matter of fact, I have a whole lot new," I defended.

"Well, he's not available right now. You'll have to leave a message," he said.

"OK, but before you transfer me to his voice mail, can I please get your name?" "Ron," he quipped hatefully.

"Ron *who*?" I inquired.

"Just Ron!" he barked.

"Ron, you don't have a last name?" I bantered.

"Nope. Just Ron." His sarcasm was mystifying.

"Boy, you guys are really professional down there, aren't you? Well, thanks, Ron. By the way, I am taping this," I gibed.

He went into a rage, cursing me and telling me that I couldn't tape him, that it was illegal.

"Why, sure I can," I calmly replied. "I've already checked with my attorney." Which was true.

Without transferring me to Dr. Yager's voice mail, Ron-with-no-last-name hung up on me.

I straight away re-dialed the Medical Examiner's number. The same young lady answered the phone. "OK, let's try this again," I challenged. "I'd like to make an appointment for my husband and me with Dr. Yager."

Now she was very polite. I was transferred to Dr. Yager's voice mail. I left a courteous and detailed message, asking Dr. Yager to please call me at his earliest convenience. I never got a reply.

I asked Bill to set in motion the process to get Richie's body in front of Dr. Newell. I was poised for battle.

Chapter 8

Message From An Angel

On Sunday following Thanksgiving Day, Larry and Olivia went to the corner market and bought a fresh-cut Christmas tree. Larry painstakingly placed the tree in the stand that he had fetched from the basement closet where it had been stored from the December before. The tree was beautiful, but my heart ached when I looked at it. Bittersweet memories from the previous Christmas flooded my mind. I retreated to my private bathroom, closed the door, buried my face in the sink, and convulsed as my tears bathed the porcelain fixture.

I wept for Richie….I wept for myself. I wept for all the Christmases that would never be again. I wept for the frightened little boy that had soiled his pants long after he should have been potty trained. And mostly I wept that he had been born to a young, single mother who had run short of patience with him in those days, not understanding the hell he was in. I saw myself standing over a 4-year-old, scorning him as I made him wash out the smelly contents of his own underwear in the toilet — a chore he had despised. This would break him, I had reasoned.

"Oh, God, why did he have to bear the burden of *my* sin?" I cried. "All I ever did was hurt him!"

I spent most of that night reduced to tears. By morning I was spent. I called my boss and told her I needed to take a leave of absence from work, I felt like I was drowning. She and I agreed that I would return the Monday following Christmas. That way I could "get through the holidays."

Larry had brought up the plastic tubs containing all the decorations I had bought the year before. He had stacked them neatly next to the tree in the corner of the living room.

I had no desire to open the boxes, but I knew I couldn't give in to my grief. My other children needed a joyous Christmas now more than ever. So, alone at home, I rummaged through Larry's tool chest in the garage and found the pruning shears.

I set out to follow a certain ritual that I apply when decorating a Christmas tree, one that requires setting the lighted top in place first. I began opening boxes in order to locate the beautiful golden-dressed angel that had adorned the top of the tree the previous year. But, much to my dismay, I didn't find it among the decorations.

Larry must have missed a box, I thought to myself. I headed to the basement storage closet to retrieve it. But I came up empty.

I dialed Larry's cell phone.

"Babe, I've lost my angel." As the words came out of my mouth, I thought of how symbolic my statement was.

Larry assured me that he had placed all the Christmas decorations that we owned in the living room next to the tree. I was puzzled by what could have happened to the angel. I searched through every other closet of our home, but it was nowhere to be found.

When Larry returned from work that evening, he did some searching himself, to no avail. After three days of literally taking the house apart, we concluded that the angel would not be found.

The Christmas tree had set bare all this time, so I decided it was time to go back to the store where I had bought the missing angel and purchase another one.

I was delighted to see several rows of lighted angel tops before me, from floor to ceiling. As I scanned the shelves, my eyes stopped at an exquisite golden-haired angel in a white gown on the top shelf. Its wings and gown were trimmed in shiny gold; it was perfect.

I stood on the tip of my toes and stretched my arms to grasp the angel and lower it into my arms. I wanted a closer look.

As the angel was descending toward me, secured loosely, it rocked forward and slammed face first into the front of the hard plastic container in which it was housed. When I got it in front of me, I was disappointed to see a white powdery residue coating the inside of the top of the container that indicated the top of the angel's porcelain head had been scarred from previous jarring.

"Oh, no," I whispered to myself. This angel was by far my favorite. "I will just have to find another one that is identical."

I was surprised to see, upon closer inspection, that each angel was unique. There were no two alike. I was astonished, because I would have thought they would have come from an assembly line in some factory somewhere.

I'll just have to find another one I like as well as this one, I surmised.

But after viewing the angels over many times, I concluded that no other angel was nearly as majestic as the angel with the wounded head. So I lowered the golden-haired angel from the top shelf to inspect it once again….and once again it rocked forward in its package.

I wonder how deep the scarring goes, I pondered to myself. The package was sealed all in one piece, so I wasn't able to open it to check the head more closely.

Finally, I convinced myself that the angel was worth taking a chance on. After all, people would be looking up at it. They would never notice if the top of its head wasn't perfect. Besides, maybe the store would discount it since it was damaged — and since I was going to be missing a month from work, a lower price would be easier on my budget.

I carried the angel to the checkout stand. A young girl was manning the cash register, flanked by a young boy who was obviously flirting with her, seemingly to her dismay. He was an off-duty employee who was spending his free time hanging around her station.

"I found this angel back in your Christmas department. I like it better than any of the others, but it's damaged. If I take it, would you be willing to discount it?" I inquired of the girl.

Before she could answer, 'Romeo' exclaimed, "Oh, yeah, they'll give you 10 percent off."

I thought that didn't sound like a whole lot, but I agreed to accept it.

The girl told me she'd have to page the shift manager in order to plug the discount into her computer....and she explained that I'd most likely have to wait a bit, because the shift manager was the only clerk on duty over at the Customer Returns desk.

As she lingered I decided to expedite the wait time by readying my payment.

Let's see, the price is $19.99 minus 10%; that would be roughly $18.00 plus tax, I calculated in my mind.

I checked my wallet to see that I had only $14.80 in cash. I was going to have to write a check. I removed my checkbook from my purse and began filling out everything other than the amount.

After what seemed like hours, the young shift manager finally came bounding over and entered her key into the cash register and punched a few keys. She then returned her key to the belt around her waist and scampered off. The cashier could now finish the transaction.

"That will be fourteen dollars and eighty cents," she announced.

"That's great!" I declared. "I won't have to write a check after all. I have exactly that much in my purse."

I voided my check, handed her the cash, retrieved the angel, and headed toward home. Obviously, the discount had turned out to be much better than 10%, but even with my math degree I was unable to appraise what percent discount she had given me with figuring in a sales tax rate of 8.35%, and I couldn't find my receipt — but the discount was roughly 32%.

When I cut the plastic container away from the angel and dusted off its head, I realized that its wound had only been superficial. The cleaned head didn't show any signs of trauma. *Perfect,* I thought, and placed my new angel at the top of the tree.

Later that evening I phoned LaRetha to catch up on the events of the day. I told her about my angel ordeal.

"Tell me you haven't missed the symbolism of this," came her reply.

"What do you mean?" I asked.

"OK, so, you lost your angel. And in its place you got a little angel with a wounded head. And the fact that the angel's head was wounded resulted in something good happening. Maybe God is trying to tell you something."

Maybe He is, I contemplated. *Maybe He is…hmmm.*

I re-visited Psalm 27. This time verse 13 spoke. I was going to "see the goodness of the Lord in the land of the living." God was going to bring something positive from this gut-wrenching ordeal….and I would not despair.

The one part of the symbolic message that LaRetha and I both missed at that time was the *long wait* before the blessing. But we should have known. After all, Psalm 27 ends with, "*Wait* on the Lord; be of good courage, and He shall strengthen your heart; *wait*, I say, on the Lord!" Little did we know just how long the wait would be.

But the one part of the message that I definitely got – God had taken my little angel out of his package and his head was healed, but the earthly shell he had left behind had an injured head....and I had to find a way to *prove* it.

Chapter 9

A Plain Path

Verse 11 of Psalm 27 says, "*Lead me* in a plain path because of mine enemies." (KJV) I was led.

First stop, headquarters of the ambulance company that had responded to the 9-1-1 call. A copy of the 9-1-1 tape and the medical records made by the EMTs who had attended Richie verified that mention was made of Richie's wreck from the outset of the ordeal. This information would become vitally important as I was led further down the path.

A reading of the records revealed some unknown facts. Richie had been given electric shock twice in order to re-start his heart. There was also a note made by the team scribe that "emesis containing pill fragments" had been observed in the stool. This was of particular interest. For instance, how many pill fragments had been seen? What was their precise condition? How digested were they? I was looking for clues that would help put together a time line of Richie's final hours — how long he had been down. Unfortunately, my request for an interview with the team scribe never received a response. (Later, in his deposition, he testified that he had made the note about the pill fragments as a 'late entry' onto the chart; the best he could recall is that one of the firemen who rode along on the ambulance to the hospital told him about them. The mystery remains.)

Next stop, KCPD East Patrol Division. I needed a copy of the police report. Surprisingly, no report had been filed since Richie was technically alive when he had left in the ambulance, and no evidence of foul play or suicide had been observed by the two officers who had responded that afternoon.

After learning the names of the officers, I first reached the junior officer. When asked if he had observed emesis in the stool, he said he had not looked at it. He explained that he had been asked by the senior officer to go find a small plastic bag in which to place the pill bottles that had been found in Richie's bathroom. He denied having been aware of any scent of alcohol on Richie's person or in the area of Richie's room; he stated that he had never been up real close to Richie but that he had not detected the smell of any alcohol in the house.

"How's your son doing?" he queried.

"He didn't make it." That was the plain, however painful, truth.

The officer seemed surprised. "Well, we should've received a call from the hospital to come back in and investigate. Any unnatural death requires the police department to conduct a full investigation," he declared.

As far as I knew, the hospital only called the Medical Examiner.

"But the ME is required to call us as well." The officer stated that he would run a check of the East Patrol Division's database to determine if a call had come in on the Sunday night that Richie had expired and promised to call me as soon as he had the results.

In the meantime, I reached his senior officer, Sgt. Rauzi. I repeated my question as to whether he had observed emesis in the stool. He said he had made a point to look in the stool, and he described seeing only something that he said one might think of as "globs of oil" floating on the water. He denied flushing the stool and said he didn't know of anyone who did. I wondered why Larry and I never saw anything out of the ordinary in the stool. Since I had never gotten to speak to the EMT who had made the reference to the pill fragments I couldn't be sure that he didn't flush the stool, but I found it difficult to believe that he would have. I could only assume that whatever had been there had melted away.

A little later the junior officer phoned back to offer some insight as to why the department was not notified by the coroner of Richie's death. He had learned that the one cause of unnatural death a Missouri Medical Examiner can rule someone without turning a case back to the police for investigation is….*suicide. How convenient,* I held, especially since neither of the officers had ever been contacted by the Medical Examiner's office to provide their observations.

I placed a call to the ME and asked to speak to Ashley. I pressed her hard to answer some questions for me…why had their office ruled Richie a suicide when it was becoming crystal clear that they had done absolutely no inquiry into the facts, and, specifically, why had Richie's wreck been totally ignored?

Ashley and I were making some real headway until she let slip a tidbit of information that evidently was supposed to be a secret: "Well, they went down to O'Toole's."

I caught my breath. "Oh, yeah? And what did *they* say?"

"Just a moment, I'll have to look in the chart," she remarked.

But that never happened. Just about that time a stern female voice came on the line and shut the call down cold – "Ashley is not talking to you anymore; good day."

Red flags were suddenly flying at full staff in my mind.

By early December 2003, I was growing impatient with Bill's slow handling of the exhumation. I was hoping to get everything settled while I was off work, so I took matters into my own hands. I phoned the funeral home in Duncan, Oklahoma, that had handled Richie's burial and told them I needed to exhume his body, asking what procedure was required. They told me they could handle everything. They would fill out a form, which would have to be signed by the public health official of the county where he was interred as well as next of kin, and then the form would be mailed to Oklahoma City to the State Health Department for final approval.

I wanted to expedite the process, so I phoned LaRetha in Texas to see if she could make the two-hour trip to Duncan, pick up the form from the funeral home, who had already arranged for the county health official's signature, take the form to Mike Patterson, who could sign it as next of kin, then drive another two hours to hand carry it into the Oklahoma State Health Department at Oklahoma City. She assented. I called ahead and the State Health Department agreed to meet her and take care of what they needed to do immediately, so she could return it to the funeral home the same day.

Meanwhile I had tried to coordinate Dr. Newell and the funeral home being able to work together so that the second autopsy could take place at their facilities in Duncan. I asked Dr. Newell about flying to Duncan, autopsy tools in hand, to examine Richie's body. She was uncomfortable with the idea, however, for several reasons....she didn't think it would be convenient to carry all of her tools on a commercial airliner; she had two small children at home which would have to be cared for by her husband in her absence, and he had other commitments; plus her father was dying, and she didn't want to be a long distance away if something were to happen to him.

To make things easier Dr. Newell checked with a transport service she was aware of to see what they would charge for two round trips to Duncan – to retrieve Richie's body, then to return it. The price was reasonable, so she called me with the idea that bringing Richie's body back to Kansas City might be the best way to go about things, and I concurred. Dr. Newell refused any payment for herself, so all I had to pay was the transport fee and a fee to the funeral home to cover the supervision costs of the vault company.

The owner of the transport company told me he would leave on the evening of Tuesday, December 9, 2003, and drive through the night to reach Richie's grave the following morning, then immediately head back to Kansas City. An unusually severe ice storm hit Tuesday evening, however, so just a few miles out of town the driver turned back. He wasn't able to head out again until two evenings later on Thursday, December 11. The following afternoon, Friday, December 12, Richie's body was delivered to Kansas University Medical Center and Dr. Newell made plans to begin the second autopsy the following morning on Saturday. During the night Friday, however, a vicious snowstorm blew in, so Dr. Newell postponed the examination of Richie's remains to the following Monday morning, December 15.

Between Friday and Monday I had an extremely difficult time emotionally. I was told by the owner of the transport company that KU Med had refused to let Richie's body be brought into their morgue facilities in a coffin, so at the last minute the transport company had had to pull some quick strings to get a local funeral home to hold the casket while they transferred Richie onto a gurney that would be accepted by the hospital. That entire weekend every time I would fall asleep, I would dream that I was going to KU Med to check on Richie. And in every case I would be turned away. It was horrifying to know that my son whom I had buried three months earlier was now lying across town, and I couldn't go to him.

That Sunday I was leaving Englewood Assembly following evening service. The cold, dark December night caused me to quicken my pace as I exited the rear doors of the church building. I scurried past three people huddled together in the middle of the parking lot as I made my way to my car.

Just as I was placing my key into the driver's side door, the voice that I had now come to know said, "Go back." As I had passed the three individuals that were engaged in deep conversation, I had overheard something being said about a lamp.

Just a few weeks before Richie's death, he had gone to Target and bought himself a nice bedside lamp. It had a touch-type on and off switch, with three levels of brightness. I had long since allowed Richie's siblings to choose from his personal belongings for items they wanted as keepsakes, but no one had been interested in his lamp. I had pondered on several occasions what to do with the lamp but had never seemed to find just the right person to give it to.

"I apologize for interrupting, but did I hear someone saying something about a lamp?" I looked into the faces of an elderly couple that attended our church, along with the mother of our evangelism pastor. The couple was inquiring of the pastor's mother about whether any lamps ever passed through the church's outreach center. Having volunteered at the center myself on a regular basis, I knew I had never seen any lamps donated.

The couple explained that a friend of theirs, a fairly young man with severe diabetes, needed a lamp. His eyesight had degenerated due to his disease, and he was having difficulty seeing how to get to the bathroom in the middle of the night. His lamp had quit working, and he was destitute and unable to afford another one.

"My son that just passed away three months ago left a nice lamp that I will be happy to give him. Just tell me where to take it, and I'll get it to him tomorrow."

The elderly woman began to weep. "Oh, ma'am, you just don't know how happy that will make him."

Her husband agreed, adding, "We live close by. Just bring it to our house and we'll get it to him." He gave me the address which was only a couple of miles from my home, and I told him I would see him the following day.

On the drive home I began to agonize about what I had just done. *Why did I promise a complete stranger one of my most prized possessions? The lamp was one of the last things Richie ever bought, and he will never purchase anything else.*

Just as I started to succumb to waves of regret, the voice said gently, "Don't sorrow about giving the lamp away. It's what Richie would want." My mind was at once settled.

I awakened the next morning with eager readiness; I bided each moment anticipating a call from Dr. Newell. I knew that she would be starting the second autopsy early that day. But the day wriggled by, and as the afternoon came the phone still hadn't made a sound.

I remembered my promise to deliver the lamp, and at the same time I was afraid to leave the house for fear that I would miss Dr. Newell's call. Finally I punched in her number and left a message on her voice recorder. "Dr. Newell, I have to run out for a few minutes, but I will be right back. Please, if you call and miss me, wait a little bit and try again. I most definitely want to talk to you before you leave for the day!"

I grabbed the lamp and hurriedly drove to the address I had been given the evening before — a humble, tidy little house where I was met at the door by the elderly man.

"One lamp," I said as I extended it toward him.

"Oh, my, this is a nice lamp! I didn't know it would be so nice! Thank you so much," he said as his hand joined mine on the lamp.

I couldn't concentrate on what he was saying, though, because the voice had returned.

"Richie will now provide light to others."

I suddenly became aware that I was lingering about releasing the lamp into the man's hand. I had been momentarily caught up into another realm. I jerked my hand back, said a quick, "You're welcome," and dashed back to my car. The man probably deemed my behavior odd, but I didn't want him to see the tears that were spilling from my eyes.

I had no inkling what the message from the voice meant, but I was more positive than ever that Richie's death was no meaningless coincidence.

That evening my mind was whirring, reflecting on all the events that had occurred since the day we had found Richie and how the voice had guided me, when I was suddenly startled by the phone. I raced to pick up the receiver and was jubilant to hear Dr. Newell's voice.

"Jennifer, I haven't completed all of my examination of your son yet. I should be able to finish and release his body tomorrow. All I can tell you right now is that I found an abnormal collection of blood in the lower right side of the back of his head, and my focus now will be to find the source of the bleed out. I will call you again tomorrow when I know more." Something about the tone of her voice consoled me. And even though she didn't have much substance to relay, I just knew she was onto something. Sleep pretty much evaded me that night.

When Dr. Newell's call came in the following evening, my spirits fell low. She hadn't been able to locate the point from where the collection of blood had originated, so she was embarking on a painstaking task that would require a long wait. She had removed sections of the back of Richie's skull from both the left and the right sides so that she could examine the entire course of all the blood vessels that were threaded through and encased in the bone of these sections of his skull. This required placing the skull sections in dishes of decalcification solution, which in time would reduce the consistency of Richie's young, dense bone to the consistency of butter. This would allow Dr. Newell to isolate the vessels from the bone without damaging the delicate material of which the vessels were comprised.

Richie's body was being released for pickup by the transport company, but it would be many weeks before I would have the answers I so desperately awaited.

Many more nightmares ensued. The conversations I had had with Dr. Newell about her worries as to whether Richie's body might have too strong an odor to house in KU Med's morgue, to now knowing that my son's head had been sawn into chunks and was lying across town in lab dishes took a great toll on my physical and emotional well-being.

Once again I clung to the portion of the 27th Psalm that said, "I would have despaired unless I had believed that I would see the goodness of the Lord in the land of the living." (NASB) Only God knows the cocoon in which He had to wrap me to keep my mind in the realm of sanity during those days.

The owner of the transport company was unable to pick Richie's remains up until the day following Dr. Newell's release. During the overnight hours of Wednesday, December 17, 2003, Richie's body was once again traveling to the cemetery in Oklahoma to be laid to rest.

I drove to my mother's house during the day on Wednesday so that I could be present the following morning for his re-burial. At approximately 10:00 AM on Thursday, December 18, I was joined by LaRetha next to the pile of earth that was waiting to be replaced over the casket in which Richie's body had been re-laid before leaving Kansas City.

LaRetha and I shivered from the cold as we watched the transport mini-van make its way into the cemetery. Two men climbed out of the front seat, and as they went around and opened the back doors of the van, they were joined by the cemetery custodian and the funeral home director.

After the four men carried Richie's casket over and set it down next to the grave, the funeral director invited LaRetha and me to take a walk over behind his vehicle. He described to us a situation that made me feel sick to my stomach. During the exhumation process the vault company had required that the cemetery custodian dig an extra wide swath with his backhoe to avoid damaging the vault. Now the funeral home's lift, that would normally span the opening of the grave during burial and be used to gently lower the casket into its resting place, was not wide enough.

"I'm afraid this is not going to be as dignified as we'd like," the funeral director apologized. He insisted that we remain with him at a distance, looking away as the remaining three men had to drop Richie's casket into the six-foot-deep hole.

I agreed, but demanded they allow me to read the 27th Psalm over Richie's casket before they re-earthed it. In retrospect, I realize this wasn't the greatest of ideas.

As LaRetha and I peered into Richie's grave, all we could see were cold, dirt walls leading down, down deep to the level at which the lid of his casket faced up toward us. I was overwhelmed with the reality of the harshness of death. At the first service there had been beautiful velvety green drapes spread around so that neither dirt nor hole could be seen. The first burial had been handled in a tasteful and refined manner; this day was different. I was shaken.

My voice trembled as I quickly read Psalm 27. When I reached the 6th verse I read, "And now my head..." I stopped. Then I began again, with more determination, "My *head* shall be lifted up above my enemies…" I glanced at LaRetha. I didn't have to tell her what I was thinking.

When I reached the end of the Psalm, I mustered all the strength I could find to look into that dark hole in which I was about to leave my son and whisper, "Bye, bye, Richie. Mommy loves you."

As we walked away my legs turned to jelly. I held onto LaRetha, once again burying my face into the chest of this beautiful human being God allowed me to have as my big sister, and I cried. I cried loud. I didn't care who heard. "Richie. Richie. Richie," I wailed.

When LaRetha and I got back to my mother's house, Mom pointed out something that had come as a startling revelation to her. "I just can't believe how these dates have worked out," she said. She had realized that Richie had made his first trip to the hospital back on Friday, September 12, and he had been delivered to the hospital again, for the second autopsy, on Friday, December 12. His first autopsy had taken place on Monday, September 15, and the second one on Monday, December 15. His first burial had been on Thursday, September 18, and now he had just been re-buried on Thursday, December 18. Two acts of God had caused this weird phenomenon. This only caused me to believe more strongly than ever that some sort of order was playing out in a universe that I could not see; things were going according to some divine plan.

Two months and five days later, after many phone inquiries and an exhausting and tormenting wait, on February 23, 2004, I received a phone call from Dr. Newell. All of the bone had finally been carefully removed from the entirety of the blood vessels from the back of Richie's head, and upon careful microscopic examination Dr. Newell had failed to find the source of the blood she had found. I was heartsick. What did this mean? Dr. Newell assured me that it wasn't necessary for her to be able to find the source in order to name "trauma" as the cause of Richie's death. She had just been hoping to find it in order to strengthen her case against Dr. Gale's verdict, and hopefully convince him to change Richie's death certificate from "Suicide." But I wasn't sure he would. I have no doubt she could sense my disappointment.

Three days later, however, things changed. On February 26, which was Hadley's 26th birthday, I received a much different call from Dr. Newell. "Jennifer, are you sitting down? I have found something. I can tell you exactly what killed your son, and there is absolutely no doubt."

I caught my breath as I sank into the nearest chair. "What?!"

Dr. Newell relayed to me how dissatisfied and frustrated she had been at the time she had called me three days earlier. "That night I was lying in bed, and I thought, 'Based on where I found the collection of the blood, if I could just examine the vertebral artery a little higher up, in the section where it attaches to the brain, I think I might be able to solve this puzzle.' It then occurred to me that we had retained your son's brain. So I went and got it and turned it over, and *there it was!*"

"There *what* was?" I was at full attention.

Dr. Newell detailed for me a clot she had found in the right vertebral artery of Richie's brain. And I'm sure she explained how she knew it had formed before death and that it would have caused death, but I didn't catch a whole lot of it. I was too busy dancing and crying and thanking God — all at once.

"It makes perfect sense that your son was taking pain medicine," she said. "He would have had an excruciating occipital lobe *headache*."

She also told me about seeing markers that indicated Diffuse Axonal Injury, also known as *shaken baby syndrome*.

Hmmm, I thought, *she sounds just like Dr. Gale sounded on September 17, 2003. Strange. Very strange.* The proverbial plot was thickening.

Dr. Newell concluded by saying, "God was with us, because even though the left vertebral artery had already been removed and was absent from the brain, the right one was still there and in pristine condition."

She seemed to think it was unusual that Dr. Gale wouldn't have already examined the right vertebral artery. The fact that the left one was gone would indicate that he most probably had dissected it for microscopic inspection.

Dr. Newell meticulously compiled an autopsy report, complete with microscopic as well as ordinary magnification pictures of her findings, and on a sunny day in March, she placed a call to Dr. Gale.

She would later relate to me that Dr. Gale's response was rather "curious."

"It was like talking to a wall," she explained. She had gone into great detail for him of her procedural steps and observations. However, he had remained so silent she had begun to wonder if he was still on the other end of the line. "Any other time I have conferred with a fellow pathologist about such a matter, I have been asked many questions – for example, 'how much, what color, how old' — in reference to blood or injuries I have found. Finally, I asked him if he had any questions or comments about anything I had said, and his response was, 'No, just send a copy of your report to my office,' gave me the address, and said, 'Good Day.'"

He didn't need to ask any questions, because he already knew what Dr. Newell had seen. He had seen it himself on September 15, 2003, and described it to me on September 17, 2003, I thought. I instantly gained a new zeal for finding out why I had been betrayed by the Jackson County Medical Examiner's office.

A few days later I placed a call to that office to inquire as to whether Dr. Newell's report had arrived. They denied they had yet received it. I double checked with Dr. Newell and learned it had been Fed-Exed across town several days earlier. I repeated my calls to the ME's office daily for two or three more days, always with the same response – "We haven't seen it."

I'll fix this problem, I decided. I drove to KU Medical Center, picked up a copy of Dr. Newell's report, and personally delivered it into the hands of the receptionist at the ME's office. As she took it from me, she promised that Dr. Gale would get it immediately. She carefully avoided making eye contact with me. I paused and stood in place silently until her eyes finally met mine. "You tell Dr. Gale I'm giving him ten days to get a correction to Jeff City," I said in a low, icy tone, my eyes burning like lasers into hers. (Jefferson City is Missouri's capital city, where all vital records are kept.) "OK," she responded nervously.

I spun, with great drama, toward the door. I was stopped by her words, however. "Ma'am, we can't totally control when it's fixed. Jeff City might take more time than that once they receive it." She sounded desperate.

"I will call Jeff City in ten days to see if they've received paperwork from Dr. Gale," I replied with grit. This time when I walked out the door of the Jackson County Medical Examiner, it was much different from the last. And this time there was no parking ticket waiting for me on my vehicle.

At 8:30 AM on April 12, 2004, still groggy from a rough night, I dialed Dr. Gale's number. The ten days had expired. When he answered, I identified myself and asked if he had gotten Richie's death certificate fixed yet. "Oh, yes!" he replied warmly, "I've already sent out the paperwork several days ago. I totally agree with KU Med's findings, and I'm very sorry about all of this."

I thanked him and hung up, finding myself once again baffled by this little man. My mind then caught a vision. *It's not him!*

Without thinking, I re-dialed his number but this time got only a voice recording. I left the following message: "Dr. Gale, I'm not sure how it was I became your enemy, but I want you to know that I don't have any hard feelings against you, because personally I don't think it was you that has put me through all of this."

As I was hanging up the phone, I was filled with wonder at how quickly my opinion and feelings toward Dr. Gale had changed. I wasn't sure how this had happened, but I was thoughtlessly aware there was someone else in the picture calling the shots.

A few days later I drove to the Jackson County Health Department and secured a copy of Richie's death certificate. I couldn't bring myself to look at it until I reached my car. As I read, "Cause of Death – Sequelae of Right Vertebral Artery Dissection, Manner of Death – Accident," I laid my head onto the steering wheel and wept uncontrollably. I had won. The emotional release consumed me.

Before pulling away I had the desire to listen to the CD onto which I had burned all the songs from Richie's services. I opened the car's console to retrieve it, but instead my fingers grasped something else — a home-burned CD that I had never seen before but that had obviously been placed there on one of the occasions that Richie had driven my car. As I lifted the CD from the console I saw on it, written in permanent marker in Richie's hand-writing, one word: *SMILE*. And I did. Because even though I didn't know why he had originally penned the message, I knew that somehow, from somewhere in the portals of another world, Richie was watching and he was cheering for me now.

"Something big is going to happen on Richie's birthday," I told Larry that night.

"What?" he inquired.

"I don't know."

"Then how do you know something is going to happen?"

"I don't know that either. But something is."

Three months later, the night before Richie's birthday, something did.

Chapter 10

Undaunted

At almost the precise time that Richie died, Larry Richard and Johnna conceived a child. Five months later, on the day Larry Richard arrived in Baghdad to give his part in the Iraqi war, Johnna had an Ultrasound test to determine the sex of the baby. It was the son they had dreamed of...but tragically, without explanation, he was dead in the womb.

On March 10, 2004, which would have been my Daddy's 91st birthday, I spoke at Baby Isaiah's memorial, put together once Larry Richard was able to get leave to come home. Sharing with the crowd that had gathered there that I had also buried a son just five months prior, I recounted to them the one question that I had asked of God when Richie had died: "Did Richie's life have a *purpose*?"

I wanted them to know I had repeated the same question about Baby Isaiah as I had held his fragile little body in the hospital the day he was forced from the womb, and that God had assured me He makes no mistakes, that every life has meaning, every life has purpose.

I related the dream of the blond-haired, blue-eyed boy that had visited Richie just before his death. "I think, since Richie never got to have any children of his own, that maybe Isaiah is a gift to him, someone to love and take care of in heaven." There was not a dry eye among the scores that looked back at me.

I concluded by reading a poem I had written for Baby Isaiah, the first verse of which I will disclose:

> You came to us so briefly, one might wonder what
>   the point,
> But in your brief brush with this life our hearts you
>   did anoint.
> Your tiny frame displayed for us the wonders of
>   creation,
> And caused us to behold our lives with new
>   appreciation.

Acts 17:26 says, "From one man he (God) made every nation of men, that they should inhabit the whole earth; and *he determined the times set for them and the exact places where they should live.*" (NIV, emphasis mine)

God orchestrates our lives; I was beginning to know this as surely as I know I exist. But by summer doubt and frustration were taking their toll.

I had aggravated Wild Bill with questions about what could be done to force an investigation into the Jackson County Medical Examiner's office, only to learn that the Medical Examiner enjoyed something called 'governmental immunity'...they could not be sued nor apparently touched in any other way. I felt dead in the water.

On July 4th weekend, 2004, I was sitting, dejected, in LaRetha's church half-heartedly listening to her pastor's Sunday morning sermon entitled "Undaunted."

"When you've done all you can to stand, then just stand. Square your shoulders and stare down the enemy. Don't budge, don't give up," the minister exhorted.

I discerned that the message was for me, but I didn't feel I had anything left to give. I had exhausted all avenues for exposing the truth.

"God, I can go no further. I've done everything I can possibly do, and I've gotten nowhere. There's no one to help; no one cares. If You want something done about this, You'll have to send some help along," I whimpered.

The first help I got was His instruction to read the 27th Psalm…again. It was verse 3 that I needed now: "Though an army may encamp against me, my heart shall not fear; though war may rise against me, in this I will be confident."

I hung on the last word — *confident.*

"*Undaunted! Yes!*" I resounded.

The next help I got was on the night of July 14th, in the form of a call from Johnna. "You won't believe what just aired on Channel 5!" she exclaimed. "They did an investigative report about Dr. Gale. Isn't that the doctor that you had problems with at the ME's office?" She couldn't recall the particulars, but she had made a note of the reporter's name.

I was at my mother's house in Comanche so that I would be able to visit Richie's grave the following morning, on *his birthday.* My words to Larry were quickly in the forefront of my mind.

An attempt to contact the reporter was met with a voice answering system. Following a fitful night, I rushed to my cousin's house in Comanche the next morning where I could access a computer to view the piece on Channel 5's website.

I was speechless as I listened to the account of how the prosecutor's office in Jackson County had sent a letter to the ME's office requesting that Dr. Yager not allow Dr. Gale to work on any cases involving potential criminal litigation. Laid bare were the details of Dr. Gale's troubled past… including a DUI arrest while on his way to work in Indiana, where he had worked in the not-too-distant past. The prosecutor contended that Dr. Gale's credibility would not hold up in court and specifically requested that the need for Dr. Gale to testify as to cause of death be avoided in any cases where there was likelihood that charges would be filed.

Acquiring the prosecutor's number through Information, I told the individual who answered the phone that I'd like to have a confidential meeting with their office to discuss troubles I had encountered at the ME's office. They were interested in hearing what I had to say, so a meeting was arranged for the following Tuesday, when I would be back in Kansas City.

The doorbell rang, and I opened the door to find that, in addition to the prosecutor's investigator, an investigator for the Missouri Board of Registration for the Healing Arts was in tow. I laid out for the duo the details of all the events through which I had lived since September 12, 2003, and I expressed my belief that the ME's office had been compromised by O'Toole Automotive.

The prosecutor's investigator informed me that the means of living of both Drs. Yager and Gale had been evaluated, and that nothing seemed awry. I was pleased to learn that someone had at least considered bribery to be within the realm of possibility. So, it surprised me that he quickly shot down any notion of any 'conspiracy theories' — "I think you're grasping at straws to make sense of what amounts to nothing more than incompetence on their part." His tone made me feel as though he saw me as pitiful, which exasperated me.

"But it wasn't *incompetence* — Dr. Gale had told me exactly what killed Richie. It wasn't that he *missed* the cause of death, it's that he *lied* about it!" I protested. "There has to be a reason he did that. O'Toole Automotive is a billion dollar corporation, and they have the power and influence to get things *fixed*, if they so desired."

My pleas for the prosecutor's office to launch an investigation were met with complete apathy. Even with the information I had downloaded from the internet about O'Toole Automotive's heavy investment into the political machine of Missouri, the state in which they just happen to be domiciled, he wasn't swayed...I was just a hysterical, grieving mother. I might as well have been screaming into the wind.

When they left, the only satisfaction I had is that the investigator for the Board for the Healing Arts had asked me if I would like to file a complaint against Dr. Gale with their office, which I was more than eager to do. He left the form with me as I bade them goodbye.

I had no confidence that anything would be done about the real root of the problem, but finally by Friday I had mustered up the effort to fill in the blanks. I placed a call to the investigator that afternoon to let him know the paperwork was ready, and 30 minutes later he was at my door with his hand out.

He seems awfully anxious to get started, I reasoned.

I'm sure Bob Gaiser had given his name the first time he had come, but I didn't catch it until now. He told me that he would be in touch, and that once his investigation was completed the Board would make a ruling, and I would receive a letter stating the actions they were going to take against Dr. Gale, if any. The list of possible punishments ranged from none at all to revoking his Missouri medical license.

This time when I closed the door behind Bob I was filled with new hope. Someone with *power* cared! He could get inside the ME's office and force out some answers.

The next time I saw Bob was when he came by to conduct a full interview. He asked each of his questions and then remained unnervingly quiet as I gave each answer. I couldn't detect even the slightest hint of whether he was believing a word I was saying.

A short time after that, I learned that he was a former Kansas City homicide detective. *I wouldn't want him interviewing me if I was guilty of something,* I decided. A few times I had caught myself rambling on just to fill the air. I wondered how many crooks he had let hang themselves, with their own words, by using that tactic.

After that visit I was constantly thinking of more details which I had left out that I was sure would be of great import to Bob, and I'm sure I tormented him with my frequent calls and messages to try and augment my account of events.

In time I came to learn that Bob's wife was from Duncan, Oklahoma, the city where I was born and where Richie's last resting place had been before his funeral. This made me feel a bit more comfortable in his presence, as I sensed it gave us some connection to each other.

As Bob got into his investigation he began experiencing health problems, some of which reduced him to a hospital bed. It was as if there was a force against his being able to do his work. I began to pray for him daily.

What I had hoped would be a quick solution to my quest for answers began to drag along. By early fall a sense of despair began to set in again.

Early one evening I stood woefully in my garden thinking how difficult it is to ride a train that is taking the long, slow route and to possess no power to speed it up. As these thoughts were passing, I looked up at an old maple tree that was giving up its leaves for winter.

"Don't fret," the voice said. "The leaves on that tree are countless, yet even though they fall one by one the huge tree will eventually be naked. That's the way this case will be. The lies will fall away one by one, and someday the truth will be exposed." I could only hope that I would have the fortitude to endure that long.

Late on the afternoon of October 19th, 2004, I visited Wild Bill. He appeared uncharacteristically aloof and disinterested. Was he starting to waver in his devotion to help me? I left his office with a sense of panic.

As I departed downtown Kansas City to engage in the drive home, my mind wondered back to the day I had driven a similar route – the day I had gone to find out why Richie wouldn't wake up. I remembered vividly having been drawn up for a moment by the message from the radio, the message that had since sustained me through some hellish days and nights.

I wonder what might be playing on KLJC that would help me get through now? I reflected.

The national elections of 2004 were only a couple of weeks away, and I had been tuning in to see what predictions all the talk radio hosts were making. But I switched the dial over just in time to hear Kristy Starling's sweet voice singing, "On the days I feel like I've failed You, the days I feel I've been failed, *I need to praise You*, for I am Yours, *I'm still Yours*. And I know You'll lead me to something more."

Another river of tears flowed from me. Mountains of anxiety melted into troughs of praise for the One who had inspired a shepherd boy thousands of years before to write down for me exactly what I needed to know.

My heart prayed verses 4 and 5 of the Psalm that was becoming such a conduit of communication from my Maker:

> "One thing I have desired of the LORD, That will I
>   seek:
> That I may dwell in the house of the LORD
> All the days of my life,
> To behold the beauty of the LORD,
> And to inquire in His temple.
> For in the time of trouble
> He shall hide me in His pavilion;
> In the secret place of His tabernacle

He shall hide me;
He shall set me high upon a rock."

I had no desire on earth except to do what the song on the radio instructed...I hid in the secret place and I *praised* Him. And I found the strength to carry on.

By the end of the year, I hadn't learned much new from Bob. He had been painstakingly re-tracing my footsteps, making the same stops I had made to verify all the facts as to what Richie's journey had consisted of between the day Larry had found him through his re-burial, but that was about as far as Bob had progressed. He had encountered budget fights going on between the newly elected Missouri governor and legislature, which left the Board's funding in doubt for a while – and Bob stopped in his tracks until the issues could be resolved.

It was time for me to take a more drastic step.

Chapter 11

Justice For Truth

On January 7, 2005, I filed suit against O'Toole Automotive for the death of Richie. I was not able to name the Jackson County Medical Examiner as a defendant in a suit, as would have been my desire, but at least with the suit I was filing, I now had subpoena authority—which was colossal. A jury trial was set for July 10, 2006.

Isaiah 42:3, read at Richie's services, had been brought back to my attention. I had chosen the verse for the first part, never knowing the second part would become an omen…"He will bring forth *justice for truth*." (NKJV) The *numbers* of the scripture were fascinating…42:3…423…"for 23" (Richie's age).

Another set of numbers was equally fascinating. I had sat straight up in bed one night in a cold sweat. I woke Larry as I erupted, "I know what the numbers mean!"

"What numbers?" he mumbled. "What are you talking about?"

"My *special* numbers." For more than five years I had carried close to my heart a set of numbers given to me, unsolicited, by a man in my Mom's church in Comanche. I had always known they represented a total change in the direction of my life. They were chapter and verse of three scripture references, written on a piece of paper. I had long since arranged them in the following sequence: 2, 11, 14, 18, 23, and 10.

"What do they mean?" Larry was now wide awake.

"My 2nd son had a wreck on the 11th, died on the 14th, and was buried on the 18th, at the age of 23, and the court date about it all is to be on the 10th," I stammered. "Richie's death has set my life on a different course forever. I will never again be a computer programmer."

Larry eventually went back to sleep. I didn't. I had a talk with God. I had noticed from early on that numbers were stacking up in a strange fashion in this case, especially the number 23. Richie had had his wreck on 23rd Street at age 23, in the year twenty-O-three, and the month and day he had died, 9/14, added up to 23. The universe had seemed to be converging onto number patterns.

I looked forward to the final number of the sequence – 10. I was ready to have the trial behind me.

By April 2005, Kansas City's Channel 5 was at my door. They produced a report on Richie's case that aired the night before my birthday — odd, since their original segment on Dr. Gale's problems had aired the night before Richie's birthday, 2004.

On June 16, 2005, Bob Gaiser turned in his report to the Board. The Board would be holding their quarterly meeting in July. The case would be on their docket. I was disappointed to learn that the scope of Bob's investigation had been limited such that no one at the coroner's office could be questioned about Richie's case other than Dr. Gale. Bob concluded that Dr. Gale was merely incompetent. "Now you know the whole truth," he assured me. I knew that's what he believed, but I didn't. I couldn't.

Another disappointment came when Wild Bill called to tell me my court date had been put off for a year. The new date was July 9, 2007. This messed up my interpretation of the number sequence: the 10 wasn't going to be a date, at least not the date of the trial.

A few days before Richie's birthday, 2005, Channel 5 called to ask if they could come over the following afternoon and get my thoughts on a letter Dr. Yager had mailed to the Board in defense of Dr. Gale. I agreed, then immediately called Bob Gaiser to ask what letter Channel 5 was talking about. Bob honored a request to drop off a copy of the 10-paged letter so that I could review it before being faced with questions on camera.

When I read the letter I almost went berserk. All I knew to do was call LaRetha. "He can't get away with this!" I cried out. "I won't let him!"

Dr. Yager had in essence accused *me* of killing Richie:

"Jennifer Morrison, the mother of the decedent, expressed her displeasure with the determination and Dr. Gale's autopsy report. According to her conversation with Dr. Gale, documented by Dr. Gale in an office case note, she was convinced that the accident caused his death and that Dr. Gale did not do an adequate dissection of the carotid arteries. She also felt the toxicology testing was inadequate and unconvincing.

"Dr. Gale informed me at a later time that he had asked her for an explanation of the drugs and alcohol in her son's blood. Mrs. Morrison, according to Dr. Gale, admitted that she supplied her son with the gin and the drugs. The Demerol and Vicodin had been prescribed to her previously for her chronic pain problems. During the evening of the accident she said the decedent was upset and that he complained of a headache. She said that she wanted to help reduce his pain and get a good night sleep so that he could go to work the next day. She allegedly thought the gin and the drugs would help."

The letter was so laced with lies and misinformation it seemed demented. How could this man be so barbarous? He obviously didn't feel bound by the facts. LaRetha tried to soothe me, urging me to calm myself.

I phoned Hadley and read him the letter. His attention fell to a later paragraph:

"Upon further review of this whole matter, I recognize now that I made a mistake in recommending the change in the death certificate. I do not now confess this in order to get back at Mrs. Morrison, because I mean her no ill will."

"But, Mom, if he's saying he should have left Richie's death certificate with 'suicide' on it, how is that? I thought *you* killed him." Dr. Yager had contradicted himself within his own letter.

Just as I was drifting off to sleep that night, a peace engulfed me and the voice whispered, "This is a *good* thing. He has done you a favor by putting his lies in writing."

Larry and I had just moved to a different house, so we had to clear a spot and stage a set that didn't look chaotic when Channel 5 arrived. As the tape began running, I was dead calm.

They informed me we would be on the air the evening of July 14th. "Do you realize that's the one-year anniversary of your first piece about Dr. Gale?" I asked. No, they didn't. Nor did they realize that they were about to give Richie his second birthday present from them.

On July 15, 2005, which would have been Richie's 25th birthday, the Board made their decision and placed a letter of concern into the permanent file of Dr. Thomas Hadden Gale.

Around the end of 2005 I had a revelation: I had missed an important clue contained in Dr. Yager's libelous letter. I got up and dug through my files. There it was:

"…in 2001…the family lodged a complaint to the Board against *me* (emphasis mine)…I was asked by the Board to appear in person in Jefferson City…"

That was it! Dr. Yager had been terrified that the Board would drag Dr. Gale in front of them for questioning like they had him (in a prior case that he was still whining about). *I wonder why that is,* I pondered. *Could it be that he is afraid of what Dr. Gale might blurt out under pressure?*

Maybe Dr. Yager hadn't written the letter to defend Dr. Gale at all; maybe he had written it to protect himself! But protect himself from *what*?

It was time to relocate Ashley, the young lady who had lied for Dr. Gale the day he took his walk. I had made note of her first name back in 2003, the last time I had spoken to her, but I didn't know her last name. When I called the Jackson County ME's office, however, I was told that Ashley had long since been gone. My request for new contact information was soundly rebuffed. I studied as to how I might find her.

Eventually I made a call to the transport company that had accommodated the return of Richie's body for the second autopsy; I was aware that they did a lot of business with the ME's office. The man who answered the phone had indeed remembered Ashley, and even though he didn't know her last name, he did know that she was presently working for the Jackson County Water Department.

The list of Jackson County employees is public information, so I called the Jackson County Executive's office and requested a list of Water Department personnel. When I received the list in the mail a couple of days later I was happy to see that there was only one Ashley listed…her last name was Dresden.

I called the Jackson County Water Department and asked for her. I was told that her shift didn't start until 4:00 PM. At 4:30 I walked into the Water Department office and requested to see her.

It was apparent almost from the beginning of our conversation that Ashley wanted nothing to do with me. *Why did you send me here, God?* I questioned silently. "Just stay kind and non-defensive, and keep talking," came the answer.

By the time I left Ashley, something had changed. She had asked for my number and told me she would call me at a more convenient time, then disappeared away from the window through which we had conversed.

Weeks went by, and I had all but given up hope that anything useful would come from Ashley Dresden…until one Friday morning when out of the blue I got a call from her. She unloaded a bombshell, leaving no doubt why God had instructed me to contact her.

There had been another case that was initially mishandled by the Jackson County Medical Examiner in early 2004, around the same time that Dr. Newell was waiting for Richie's bones to de-calcify. A young lady named Alisha, whose last name Ashley couldn't recall, had been brought into the ME's office for autopsy. She had been immediately ruled a drug overdose and sent to her grave.

After Dr. Newell had contacted Dr. Gale, however, a decision had been made by Dr. Yager to exhume Alisha's body — at the county's expense — for a second look. Alisha had also been involved in a minor car accident just prior to her death…and sure enough, Alisha had the same injury as Richie. Coincidentally, Alisha had also been in her grave around three months, according to Ashley. Dr. Yager had written in his letter to the Board:

"Any forensic pathologist would know that you cannot rely on findings of soft tissue hemorrhage on an embalmed body, particularly one that has had a cranial autopsy performed previously, but Dr. Newell apparently does not know this."

Ashley championed the fact that Dr. Yager's letter to the Board was a *lie*. Almost precisely a year before he penned the letter, he had spent taxpayers' money to follow the exact same procedure Dr. Newell had performed in Richie's autopsy. And Dr. Yager had corrected Alisha's death certificate!

The parallel, yet radically different treatment by Dr. Yager, of the two cases gave me pause. I left a breathless message for Wild Bill. This would change *everything*.

I looked toward the heavens and let out a war cry. God had indeed answered another mother's prayer for truth, just as He had promised. Alisha's mother now had the peace of knowing how her daughter had really died.

Ashley had also told me that the autopsy assistant that had aided Dr. Gale with Richie's autopsy had quit his position at the ME's office after 14 years of service, because he could no longer stomach some of the actions of Dr. Yager. I asked for his name, but Ashley didn't feel comfortable providing it.

Another call to the Jackson County Executive's office gave me the name: Casey Shumer. But after a great amount of Internet searching I could find no mention of Casey Shumer in phone listings. A friend suggested I try legal records, and bingo, a Casey Shumer, along with his address, appeared. There was no phone number listed, so I hurriedly drove to the address. The man who answered the door told me that he had bought the house from Casey Shumer a year earlier. He didn't know exactly where Casey had moved to, but he thought it was "somewhere just off 95th Street." At least Casey was still in town.

Property tax records, I thought. *They would reveal his new address.* In a scene reminiscent of the movie *Erin Brockevich,* I managed to get Casey's new address from the Jackson County Courthouse Tax Records department by distracting a computer operator long enough to steal a glance at his screen. Another drive landed me at Casey's front door face to face with his wife and kids.

When I explained to Casey's wife my reason for being there, her repartee was tantalizing. "Oh, you've got to come back or call when Casey's home from work. He'll be able to tell you anything you want to know about that office…and, believe me, he knows a *lot.*"

I was ripe with anticipation. I immediately left a message on his cell, the number of which she had disclosed.

When Casey finally responded, he had little time to talk. He suggested a call to another autopsy assistant named Steffan Parsons might fill in some blanks for me. Steffan had been hired to take Casey's place and had only lasted a year after being appalled by what he had observed in Dr. Yager's office — and Steffan and Dr. Yager had even been long-time friends at the time Steffan had gone to work for Dr. Yager.

I asked Casey quickly if he knew about the "Alisha" case. He recalled it, but couldn't remember her last name. He told me he could probably find out, though. We agreed to talk again soon when it was more convenient for him.

I immediately placed a call to Steffan. I got an ear full. Steffan had gone to every prosecutor in the four-county area of western Missouri for which Dr. Yager's office performed autopsies trying, in vain, to get Dr. Yager removed from office. He explained to me that the response of the apathetic officials to whom he had expressed concern was that Dr. Yager would lose his office at the end of 2006 anyway (which they considered an acceptable solution), because everyone knew that the County Executive who had appointed Yager was not going to re-run for office, due to public corruption problems of her own. (She was under investigation by the FBI.) Plus the current prosecutor was a shoe-in to win the election, and he was the one who had initially gotten Dr. Yager's office the unflattering report by Channel 5; he was certain to replace Dr. Yager.

I was suddenly hit with an exciting thought — *hey, the FBI... that's who needs to be looking at this.* I asked Steffan if he had thought of contacting them. He said no, but if I did to let them know he would be anxious to relay to them what he knew.

I began making frequent calls and trips to the FBI head-quarters in downtown Kansas City, just a block away from Argus, where I was working the day I had received the phone call that Richie wouldn't wake up. I can sum up in one word the response I got: *disinterest.* It was a dead end. My frustration level went off the charts.

One thing that always haunted the back of my mind: Both Casey and Steffan, knowing Dr. Yager well, had doubts that Dr. Yager would do anything so low as to take a bribe, which is what I was becoming convinced of at that point. He was just arrogant and rude, they said — too smart for his own good. So *who* was the culprit?

Dr. Newell's deposition was taken July 11, 2006. I was cognizant for the first time that day that Dr. Kathy Newell had been an instructor at Harvard University before she had come to KU Med's pathology department. The list of accolades contained in her curriculum vitae were beyond astonishing.

As Dr. Newell revealed to us her work on Richie's case, her teaching background was evident in her manner of presentation. Sitting in a small, stifling office, watching her bring up slide after slide on her computerized projector for the benefit of Wild Bill and O'Toole's attorney, I had trouble holding my emotions. This was the lady of whom Wild Bill had asked, "How in the world did you find *her*?" How, indeed. I was sitting now, spellbound, watching as God was weaving another row onto the great tapestry He had begun on that wretched October evening when He had instructed me to "call Mark Doherty – he'll tell you what to do."

When asked to address Richie's toxicology report, Dr. Newell put on her hat as the former Poison Control Center employee. She explained that an acetaminophen level of 110 is a little high but that it doesn't take very many pills to get that level. Any acetaminophen level below 300 is not considered dangerous.

I learned that Dr. Newell had presented Richie's case to the American Association of Neuropathologists at their annual convention held in the summer of 2005 in Washington, D.C. And I learned that Dr. Newell would be introducing a paper on Richie's case into the medical literature. Dr. Newell showed us a letter she had received, dated on Richie's birthday, 2005, from the Miami Dade County, Florida, Medical Examiner, requesting pictures of Richie's injuries for use in their own office. Richie was, veritably, now *bringing light* to others.

Dr. Yager showed up for his deposition November 6, 2006, and lived up to his reputation. He was arrogant, condescending, and combative, trying to hurt me by any means possible. He attempted to pick apart Wild Bill's questions and made his deposition last at least twice as long as it should have. Not surprisingly, though, he made nothing off of Wild Bill.

Smirkingly, Dr. Yager stated that he felt he should probably go ahead and try to get Richie's death certificate changed back to 'Suicide'. Wild Bill grinned as he retorted, "You'd like to do that, Doctor, but you won't, because you know if you try to change a death certificate the second time, the statutes of Missouri provide for a full and independent investigation, and your office couldn't withstand such an investigation."

Dr. Yager was asked if he could tell the difference between a clot that formed before death as opposed to a clot that formed after death. He was hesitant to answer, knowing that his admittance that Richie's clot had formed before death would prove his untruthfulness in the remainder of his testimony. Wild Bill nailed him on it. "Doctor, if you're going to say that you can't tell the difference, I need to show the tape of this deposition to a lot of people I know, because you're going to be in some real trouble in some criminal cases you've testified in."

The last five minutes of his deposition were the best, though. Wild Bill hit him with the bombshell question: "Dr. Yager, didn't you exhume another body immediately after Mr. Patterson's case in which you had ruled another person a drug overdose and then you found that she had the same injury as Mr. Patterson and you changed her death certificate?" Talk about a deer in the headlights. It was priceless. Dr. Yager was so stunned and so unprepared he just perjured all over himself and blurted out, "No, I don't recall anything like that." Wild Bill merely smiled and said, "No further questions." Of course, O'Toole's lawyer looked as though she had been hit by a bus, because Yager was their golden boy, or so they had thought.

As Dr. Yager exited, Dr. Gale entered, complaining loudly that we had kept him waiting for an hour and a half. I wanted to tell him two things: 1) if his boss would have given straight answers he wouldn't have had to wait, and 2) maybe he now knew how I felt the day he took his hour-and-a-half "walk" after having Ashley lie for him on October 27th, 2003. God was showing his sense of humor.

The total antithesis of Dr. Yager, Dr. Gale went to great effort to be totally and completely truthful in his deposition, even giving us information we hadn't realized existed. For example, Richie not only had a vertebral artery clot but he had a brainstem injury, Dr. Gale admitted. Dr. Yager and *especially Tom Hinsley*, the investigator, had steamrolled over him in the 'Suicide' ruling, he told us.

Dr. Gale divulged vivid details of Alisha's case, including the fact that, due to it being very expensive to exhume a body and because of the extensive man-hours required to do the vertebral artery dissection like Dr. Newell had done on Richie, Dr. Yager had had to initiate the exhumation.

Yet, much to Dr. Gale's dismay, he had had to cross Dr. Yager in order to fix Richie's death certificate. Dr. Yager hadn't wanted it fixed, even while planning Alisha's exhumation. Dr. Gale didn't have a good answer for Dr. Yager's behavior – Dr. Yager just had a strong will and a mind of his own, he said.

Dr. Gale's statement about Tom Hinsley being the one who leaned on him most to name Richie a 'Suicide' brought Tom Hinsley into our sights. We subpoenaed him to deposition December 20, 2006…and the mystery got deeper.

Tom Hinsley showed up without Richie's entire case file, as had Drs. Yager and Gale in direct disregard to their subpoenas. What Tom Hinsley did show up with were some case notes he had personally placed in the file. Two of them, both dated 06/28/2006, were titillating.

On that day, just six months earlier, Chief Investigator Ron Butterfield, also known as Ron-with-no-last-name, had asked Tom Hinsley to re-check into Richie's alcohol level in relation to what time it was drawn at Independence General. Tom had requested someone there pull Richie's records from storage and see if there were any handwritten notes in the chart that wouldn't show up in the computer. Tom had also contacted a police officer to verify no BAC (blood alcohol content) had been run on Richie.

Wild Bill asked Tom why and at whose behest this investigative work had been done by the ME's office more than two years after Richie's case had been officially closed by the ME. Tom claimed to have no knowledge, he was just following Ron's orders.

Tom testified under oath that he did nothing on Richie's case between September 15, 2003, at 1:00 AM (2 ½ hrs after Richie expired) and October 15, 2003, when he tried to reach Jill. He couldn't name *anything*, ever, he did, other than make phone calls, to investigate Richie's death. He –

- Never tried to verify the level of drugs or asked to look at the bottles
- Never tried to talk to the police officers who worked the death scene
- Never tried to reach the EMTs or firemen that were involved
- Never tried to talk to the ER doctor
- Never talked to Richie's family doctor about prescriptions
- Didn't ask if a suicide note was left
- Didn't try to find out Richie's activities the day he was found
- Never talked to Richie's employer
- Never visited the death scene or the accident scene
- Never inspected Richie's car
- Never inspected O'Toole's truck
- Never talked to John Jenkins, the other driver in the wreck
- Never talked to anyone at O'Toole Automotive

Yet, Tom Hinsley, according to Dr. Gale, was the one who pressed Dr. Gale to rule Richie a 'Suicide'. Something was wrong with this picture.

We had thought we would be through with depositions at the ME's office up until Tom Hinsley's testimony. Now we knew we needed to focus on Ron-with-no-last-name, but

Wild Bill's schedule was so full we were going to have to wait until well into 2007.

On Monday, June 18, 2007, I met Lou Accurso and Wild Bill at Wild Bill's office. They wanted to talk to me about sending a demand letter. Lou said he had researched jury verdicts in our county, and juries were giving an average of $750,000 in cases like Richie's, with some much lower, so he thought asking for somewhere between $750,000 and a million dollars would be good for me. I told him I wasn't ready to do that. I could tell he wasn't pleased. He asked if we could at least agree to talk about it again four days later, on Friday. "Sure," I said, "we can talk about it."

On Wednesday four of us – Wild Bill, Lou, Lou's investigator and I — went to see Ashley Dresden at the Jackson County Water Department. She recalled having a lengthy phone conversation with me, she even named Denise Daughtry as the one who had disconnected us, but she had no specific recall of telling me "they went down to O'Toole's." She didn't deny she had said it, she just no longer remembered – which was enough for Lou.

Just before we had headed from Lou's office to see Ashley, Lou and I had had a private talk about whether anyone else would ever benefit from knowing what was done to Richie. He advised me that any other family's problems with the Jackson County ME's office were "outside the scope of this case." He told me that I was extremely lucky to know what "truth" I knew, and that I only knew that much because of my tenacity. I told him I am not lucky, that I have a big God. He was visibly uncomfortable.

On Thursday we went to the ME's office. Denise Daughtry was at a funeral for her aunt in Iowa, so Ron-whose-last-name-was-Butterfield was the only one present to depose. And he was not happy. He callously threw Richie's case file onto the table in front of Wild Bill. This time it was the entire file.

As Wild Bill thumbed through it two handwritten notes fell out, penned by Ron. One of the notes said, "Bill for Tom Hinsley 4 hours, Dr. Gale 1 hour." It was attached to the business card of Keith Voltaire from Sherman, Tucker and Kilman. The other note said "Carrie Berne @ Landrop and Gore", along with Carrie's phone number. Ron said this second note was in conjunction with having Tom Hinsley go back to Independence General in the summer of 2006 to poke around some more into Richie's case…he said he wanted to make sure that the ME's zero level alcohol finding was correct, because Landrop and Gore had pointed out that it didn't match the one at Independence General.

Bill asked why none of the time spent with Keith Voltaire or at Independence General on O'Toole's behalf was billed out, like they had billed us. Ron had no explanation, claiming that the first note probably didn't even belong in Richie's file.

He wanted to dispel any notion that he had done any special favors for O'Toole Automotive. He said his office would re-check something even if "the bum on the street" called to tell them they had gotten something wrong.

"Well, when Mrs. Morrison called to tell you there were things you were missing in this case, you *hung up* on her! Wasn't she as good as the bum on the street?" Wild Bill fired at him.

I took note that Ron was sweating profusely the entire time of questioning, mopping his face and bald head with a hand towel. I felt that he was anxious to the point of physical illness. I wondered why answering a few simple questions should be causing him such distress.

After the deposition Bill called Keith Voltaire, who denied having met with Tom Hinsley or Dr. Gale about "the Patterson case." He said he had met with them, but it was on another case, the "Bryce" case.

Friday came and went without any talk of the demand letter.

The following Tuesday Wild Bill called me and begged, practically, to be able to send a demand letter for $2.5 million. I was still hesitant at first, because I was terrified they might pay it and my subpoena power would evaporate, but then I finally and suddenly agreed. As soon as I said OK, a huge weight lifted off of me. It was as if I had been able, at last, to let go of control of the case for the first time. Wild Bill seemed greatly relieved, but it wasn't him that I felt I had released the case to, it was God.

By evening I heard the voice say, "Go back and find the scripture from the three whose references you've held onto for years that says something about, 'Now, I will do what I promised you...'"

I had spent a considerable amount of time searching when I came up with it. It was Numbers 11:23 – the book of the Bible was even *called* "Numbers."

"Is the Lord's power limited? Now you shall see whether My word will come true for you or not."

I was about to see awesome things. Beautiful things. I was about to see the arm of God.

Chapter 12

My Head Is Lifted Up

The Honorable Judge Marco Roldan introduced the jury panel to a frigid courtroom on July 9, 2007. He warned them that if they were selected to serve on the case of Morrison v. O'Toole Automotive Inc. they might want to bring a jacket with them each day, as the air conditioning in the 16th Circuit Court of Missouri tended to drive out any allusion of warmth.

Just as the trial was about to begin, we were informed that Dr. Mary Case, a neuropathologist from St. Louis who O'Toole Automotive had paid to review Richie's case, wasn't going to testify that Richie's death was caused by anything other than the wreck. This left them with no expert witness to counter Dr. Newell's findings.

As the Plaintiff's presentation of evidence began, Dr. Newell took the stand. With words, diagrams, and slides this former Harvard instructor painted a vivid picture for the jury as to why Richie Patterson is no longer on the earth. The jury liked her. They understood her.

She informed them that after she had consulted with Dr. Gale about her autopsy findings that he had produced for her some further work he had done from his retained tissue samples, and that he had found the source of Richie's clot – a dissection in the right vertebral artery.

Mr. Gary Landingham, O'Toole Automotive's lead attorney, buffeted Dr. Newell for her "science fair" display in Washington, D.C., and her medical journal paper produced about Richie's case, and for the fact that this was her first post-interment autopsy. But she never faltered. His rudeness and belittlement were met with the courtesy and grace of a true professional.

She was followed by a high-tech accident reconstructionist who testified that the damage he measured on both the O'Toole Automotive Chevy S-10 pickup and Richie's Toyota illustrated that Richie had established himself eastbound in the center lane of 23rd Street at a time when the O'Toole Automotive driver was still parked at the stop sign. This opinion fastened the blame for the collision squarely onto the driver of the O'Toole pickup.

Sworn in next was Dr. Barry Jeffries, a neuroradiologist, who testified that the clot that killed Richie had formed upstream, then broken loose to clog a vessel that was no thicker than a couple of human hairs. His testimony was the most difficult to receive. He verbalized possible symptoms that Richie may have experienced as he was dying, driving a dagger through the core of my heart as he spoke.

Wayne Hice, Vice President of Risk Management for O'Toole Automotive, listed his job duties as "taking care of our corporate assets, protecting our team members, protecting the public and our assets." He stated that records of lawsuits and claims and collisions involving O'Toole vehicles are kept under his oversight, within 20 to 30 feet from his desk.

Mr. Hice squirmed as Lou Accurso asked him to explain why he had responded, under oath, to a case interrogatory, "Defendant states that it knows of no accidents involving O'Toole vehicles at or near the intersection of 23rd Street and Randall in Independence, Missouri, in the ten years immediately preceding September 11, 2003." Lou produced documents showing that, on May 26, 2000, another O'Toole driver had also been in a collision while making a left turn at that very intersection, the intersection where Richie had sustained mortal injury. Lou hammered Mr. Hice for his dishonesty.

The other party in the prior wreck had filed suit against O'Toole Automotive on a most interesting date – July 15, 2004, the first of Richie's birthdays that he had missed — and that suit remained in litigation well past the date that Mr. Hice and team untruthfully answered the interrogatory.

In other testimony, Mr. Hice claimed to have no termination report on file for John Jenkins, the O'Toole driver that collided with Richie, despite John having been let go by O'Toole on the 23rd of September, 2003, yet Mr. Hice vehemently denied that John Jenkins had been fired because of the accident.

John Jenkins described for the jury the truck that had caused Richie's death. John told of a standard shift gear stick that wouldn't go into first gear, which required bumpy take-offs from second. He described having to hold his left arm out the window whenever he was making a left turn, because the left front signal didn't work – a situation he had allegedly complained about numerous times to his supervisors without results. Following the wreck John continued to drive the truck in the same condition — other than the front bumper having been tied up with a black string after Richie's car had knocked it loose — until his termination by O'Toole Automotive 12 days later. The pickup was subsequently sold to another O'Toole driver for $250, who fixed the faulty signal light with a $2.00 bulb. The total worth of the two vehicles that took Richie's life was $500.

The City of Independence records custodian brought to court a stack of papers containing reports of 15 other wrecks in which the Independence Police had been dispatched to the intersection of 23rd and Randall. Lou and Wild Bill suggested to the jury that O'Toole Automotive should have realized that this intersection was dangerous and should have instructed their drivers to plan their routes to avoid making left turns from there, as stated in their published Safety Training Manual.

Another questionable interrogatory answer given by O'Toole Automotive was that they first learned Richie was dead in the fall of 2004, a *full year* after he was gone. When asked during the trial, the gentleman who was acting store manager at the time of the accident gave testimony that he had discussed the fact that Richie had died with the regular manager upon the regular manager's return from medical leave. And the regular manager had already declared that it was he who had fired John Jenkins *12 days* following the wreck, *just after his return* from medical leave.

Richie's Dad took his turn in front of the jurors and brought the first real tears of the trial from my eyes, tears that I was fighting hard to suppress, as I didn't want a sympathy vote for a verdict.

Mike Patterson spoke of the son that reminded him most of himself, introverted and awkward. When asked what he misses most about Richie, his answer was austere: "I miss *him.*"

A string of witnesses followed…an economist who enumerated how many lost wages Richie potentially left behind; a representative of DeVry University who laid out what opportunities Richie's degree path might have afforded him; a co-worker who lauded Richie's work ethic.

Sgt. Rauzi – the policeman who had beckoned to my 9-1-1 call – recounted finding the medicine bottles in Richie's bathroom, all with lids fastened. He opined that the scene to which he had arrived did not have the characteristics of that found in a suicide; hence, no such report had been filed by his department.

Exactly ten days after arriving home from defending his country in Iraq, Quentin stood to defend his brother's honor. Dressed in battle fatigues, Quentin reminisced of the cherished "Momma's boy" he had breached Basic Training to bury, the one who had taught him and protected him through childhood...the one who had taught his baby daughter, "Livvers" (Richie's name for her), how to walk, a daughter who now has no memory of him.

Larry somberly offered to the jury details of how he had lost his wife the day Richie died. Then, finally, it was my turn.

On July 17, 2007, I placed my right hand in the air and swore to tell the truth, the whole truth, and nothing but the truth. It was a Tuesday morning that I had given Richie life, now it was a Tuesday morning that I was contending for his right to have been alive. The irony of it was stupendous.

The Defense's strategy was simple: I had known from the beginning that my son had killed himself, but then I had seen dollar signs and decided to make something of the wreck... despite the fact they knew my 9-1-1 tape proved otherwise.

Gary Landingham led the 2 ½ hour attack. He made me feel as though he saw Richie as a simple piece of waste, the discarding of which was insignificant at most. But he stumbled...that's what many people were saying afterwards. He *stumbled*, just like Psalm 27:2 said he would.

Nothing he said could phase me, because what he didn't know is that I already had what I had come for. Just five days prior, on July 12, Wild Bill had snuck in the briefest witness of the trial — Denise Daughtry, records administrator at the ME's office. Denise verified that the notes that had fallen from Richie's file the day we had deposed Ron-whose-name-was-Butterfield *belonged in Richie's file and none other*. I didn't know *how*, but I now knew *who* had had a dog in this race that shouldn't.

The remainder of the trial I was just going through the motions, trying to appear alert and respectful to the experts called by O'Toole Automotive.

Their expert ER doctor/toxicologist said that blood could only clot when it was stopped from flowing, as in death. I facetiously thought to myself, *That's good to know, that as long as I'm alive and my blood is flowing, I can't get a blood clot. Too bad all the poor schmucks who have died of blood clots hadn't met this genius!*

Their accident re-constructionist, a blue-blood who has made millions from testifying for such clients as General Motors (whose vehicles have evidently *never* caused harm to a single person), testified that the wreck was more of a head-on collision. He insisted he hadn't relied on the police report of the accident, and it was obvious.

My personal favorite was the bio-mechanic who predicated that the impact suffered by Richie wasn't severe enough to cause an arterial dissection in Richie's head. I wanted to rise and ask him if he could please go to Fairlawn Cemetery and explain that to my son.

Their neurosurgeon didn't show up at all.

In light of the unsafe mechanical condition that O'Toole Automotive's driver described their pickup truck to be in, Judge Roldan ruled the jury could consider punitive damages – which I suspect almost caused Gary Landingham heart failure. In his distinguished career, he had never had to face the deliberation of punitives before.

Closing arguments were given, and then just before lunch on Thursday, July 19, we retired to begin the long, agonizing wait that every trial lawyer dreads. Tensions were high as the clock seemed to tick toward infinity.

While waiting in the hallway the last time the jurors reconvened, following their lunch on the second day of deliberations, I read the 27th Psalm one more time. And one last message was waiting. Verse 1b says, "The *Lord* is the *defense* of my life." *Defense*…a courtroom term. It was not the lawyers who were going to be able to take credit for the outcome…but I wasn't sure how it could be any other way.

In the 10th hour of deliberation, on the 10th day of the trial, 10 jurors signed the verdict. It was over. The last number of the sequence had been fulfilled. There would be no appeal by the defense; I didn't have to wait for the allotted 30 days in which they had to file one to know that.

The verdict was $1.2 million, with 33% fault for the wreck being assessed to Richie, for a net verdict of $804,000.

My mind went back to the Christmas angel that had replaced my lost one. The discount had been roughly 3.2 times what the store had told me they would give. O'Toole Automotive had offered $250,000…and the jury awarded me roughly 3.2 times that.

One of the jurors stayed around and talked to us. She said she wanted to award me $5 million, but the way the jury instructions were worded they were confused and thought they could only award the exact expenses (which wasn't true, but by law they weren't allowed to ask for clarification). I told her hearing that she thought Richie was worth $5 million was worth $5 million to me.

A jury of my peers had looked at the evidence from an objective viewpoint, and it was unanimous that not for one second did a single one of them believe Richie had killed himself. The reason two of them didn't sign the verdict was in protest that they couldn't give me more in damages (or so they had thought).

As the jury had filed out of the jury room to leave the courthouse and re-enter their normal existence, I handed each of them a packet containing a CD and a letter:

Dear Member of the Jury,

It is 11:30 PM on Tuesday night, July 17, 2007. I wish I could talk to you, but I cannot, so I shall write to you, knowing that you will not see this until you have reached your verdict. Whatever decision you have made in this case, please know that it is the right one.

On October 27, 2003, the day that the coroner's office informed me that Richie was going to be declared a suicide, I thought I would literally perish.

But then I was reminded of a strange passage from the Bible that I had chosen for Richie's services – Psalm 27 — and it brought me great strength. I had never understood until that day why I had been compelled to have it read over him.

On October **27**, 2003, at **12** noon, was my first realization that the entire psalm was becoming a prophecy of sorts. Psalm **27:12** says, "Deliver me not over unto the will of mine enemies, for false witnesses are risen up against me, and such as breathe out cruelty."

It would be impossible for me to tell you in this letter the details of my journey for the past 3 years and 10 months, but suffice it to say I've never been more sure that there is a God and that He cares very much about every detail of our lives.

I will tell you that several people in powerful positions no longer have those positions because of this case. I filed a suit in order to have subpoena power to force people to talk, and I have refused to settle out of court because I wanted to know the *truth*. Many people told me I would never know the truth, but I never believed them. The Psalm told me differently. The hardest part about it all was the final verse – "Wait on the Lord…wait, I say on the Lord." Wait I did, and it worked.

On Thursday, July 12, 2007, the fourth day of the trial, you may remember that Denise Daughtry, records keeper at the coroner's office, admitted under oath that everything that had been found in Richie's file belonged there. What my lawyers for some reason were not allowed to tell you is that in that file there was a business card from O'Toole's other law firm with notes confirming a meeting with the coroner's investigator assigned to Richie's case (4 hours) as well as an hour with Dr. Gale. These notes were in the handwriting of the chief investigator, Mr. Ron Butterfield. The day after Ms. Daughtry testified, and under threat of subpoena, Mr. Butterfield suddenly took early retirement from the coroner's office at age 50. (See Psalm 27:2)

I will live the remainder of this life with a handicap – I will have a part of my soul missing…anything or nothing that you have awarded me will change that. I will not have lunch with Richie tomorrow, nor 20 years from tomorrow if I continue to breathe. O'Toole's could give me their entire company, and I would still not be whole.

So, if you have chosen not to award me anything it will be of little significance to my life. I have an incredible husband, two beautiful sons, two precious daughters-in-law, and the three most adorable grandchildren that have ever been. And most of all I have a Friend that will see me through until I meet Richie again.

If you have chosen to award me something, I will do my best to be a good steward and use it to help others…what Richie would want.

Either way, I want you to have something personal from me that will express my heart. On April 6, 2006, I wrote and recorded a song, and I have made a copy for you. Please accept it as my thanks for sitting through many long (freezing!) days of testimony and arguing lawyers, and may it cause you to realize how special the people are whom God has given you to love on this Earth. ☺

Sincerely,
Jennifer Morrison

P.S. The other verse that was read at Richie's services was Isaiah 42:3. I'll let you read it. It might make you smile…especially the last phrase.

A few days later I looked up Ron Butterfield's phone number. I didn't use it, but I couldn't help noticing that his street address was on *Patterson*. O'Toole Automotive's world headquarters, where they were served their original subpoena, is also on *Patterson*. A coincidence? Maybe. Or maybe a shy, little boy named Richie *Patterson* was getting to send his mother one last clue that there is a divine order in all we suffer.

The day Ron left the ME's office, Friday, the 13th of July (a terrific early birthday present for Richie), Larry was at a BMW motorcycle shop right near the entrance of the rail yard bridge where I had briefly been drawn from reality on my way home the day Richie wouldn't wake up. Larry was curiously drawn to a bike that he initially found to be ugly. When the salesman noticed him checking it out, he told him that particular model hadn't been made since 2004, rolling off the assembly line in late 2003 (about the time Richie had died). Larry decided to get the VIN number and obtain insurance rate information in case he decided to make an offer on it. The salesman went in the store and re-appeared with a copy of the title, which, upon inspection, caused Larry to go weak in the knees. The bike was titled to a *Richard D. Patterson*. Richie's middle initial is "J," but it was close enough to get Larry's attention.

The next time I saw Lou Accurso was the day he informed me we were going to have to go back to court one last time to appropriate the damages to Richie's rightful heirs. "The hearing is scheduled for September 12th at 8:30 AM," he said.

"September 12th?! That's the day we found him, the day this all began," I gasped.

"Isn't it amazing how these things keep happening with this case?" he wondered out loud.

I spoke to Lou again that day of the God Who had accompanied me on my four-year journey. And this time Lou Accurso didn't seem the least bit uncomfortable.

Chapter 13

To Something More

To everything there is a season, a time for every *purpose* under heaven: a time to be born, and a time to *die...* (Ecclesiastes 3:1,2a – emphasis mine) This is one of the most certain truths I possess. Another is stated in Jeremiah 29:13, where God declares, "You will seek Me and find Me when you search for Me with all your heart."

My heart has found Him. And now that I have a glimpse of Him, I realize that it has always been Him for whom I've searched. Every longing for fulfillment has been a longing for His approval; every desire for intimacy a desire for His embrace; every thirst for beauty a thirst to behold His countenance. I will never again be satisfied with less. I think C.S. Lewis was experiencing a similar epiphany when he yielded, "All your life an unattainable ecstasy has hovered just beyond the grasp of your consciousness."[1]

I know now the ecstasy of which he speaks — it is what I live for. It is the peace that engulfs my soul, the enchantment that my tongue cannot articulate, the prize that is set before me. John Donne captures it as well as anyone – "No man ever saw God and lived. And yet, I shall not live till I see God; and when I have seen him, I shall never die." Lewis explains, "Until you have given up your self to Him you will not have a real self…Nothing in you that has not died will ever be raised from the dead. Look for yourself, and you will find in the long run only hatred, loneliness, despair, rage, ruin, and decay. But look for Christ and you will find Him, and with Him everything else thrown in."[2]

For years I looked for Richie. I went to the ICU where he had died; he wasn't there. I journeyed to Philadelphia where he had lived; he wasn't there. It seemed that he was everywhere, yet he was nowhere.

But I had prayed for help, and God *had* helped us. Richie had been given time…time to find the grace of God with its unconditional love and acceptance for which he had always yearned; time to acquire eternal rewards for profitable service to a kind and benevolent King; time to provide me with armament for a mind-assaulting battle that otherwise would have destroyed me; time to find his way home. All is well.

If Larry hadn't felt the tug to drop by our house at precisely the minute and second he had, there would have never been a CT scan to intrigue Dr. Newell, which means I would have never known the truth, and Richie would have never been able to contribute so much to so many. He would merely be stretched out, perhaps with me next to him, in the shadow of a tombstone, while occupying his space in the record books as another heart-breaking statistic.

But God had taken the ME's insult personal, maybe because His own son had been falsely accused by those who had caused His death. And it was God who stood last… the lawyers, brilliant and eloquent as they were, had been unable to penetrate the barrier of a seemingly foreordained outcome.

A psalm with which both ministers had struggled to find anything from which to comfort the family had become our greatest comfort.

On September 16, 2007, Larry and I attended the Missouri State CMA rally where I met Susanne Johnson, the state Web Master for CMA. Susanne was still in binding grief for her son, Daryl, who had died just before his 19th birthday three years earlier. Daryl's death had been mysterious, and there were questions whose answers Susanne hungered for.

Susanne had sobbed as I had sung "Glad You Came Along" (the song given to the jury on CD). I asked her to tell me why. She recounted how Daryl had gone into a treatment program at a clinic in Houston, TX, by his own choice; how he had called her three weeks later on a Saturday sounding terrific; how he went missing two days later and was subsequently found dead in an apartment in Chicago, Illinois. There had been little to no information provided by the police or the clinic. Medical reports? Scant. Autopsy report? Confusing. Suspects? Zero interest in looking for any.

"I don't have the strength or know-how to even fight this," she agonized.

"Help her," God whispered. "This is what you are to do now."

"I'm ready," I agreed.

Imagine how I was affected a few days into my new assignment when I realized the precise date of Daryl's death: October 19, 2004. That was the exact evening that I had sung along with Kristy Starling, "I know You'll lead me to something more."

****

Grief is like a bottle of bitter medicine. It can't be taken all at once or it will kill. It must be taken dose by dose until it is gone. If it ever is.

But, see, Richie, I always told you that everything happens for a reason. And when the storm came we remained...

because our life was built on the Rock. We were never good enough nor strong enough, but He was and is.

I do not question Him about why circumstances played out the way they did, I simply trust Him. As Rev. David George once said, "He is too kind to do anything cruel, too wise to make a mistake, and too deep to explain Himself to me." I simply rest in the knowledge that I have completed all He asked of me through this…and that final justice remains in His hands. He will continue to endow me with the strength to give what I gave, and I will never cease to worship Him for every millisecond of time he allowed you and me together on this earth. I count it an unspeakable honor and privilege that it was me He chose to be your "Mom."

I thank you for all the things you taught me and for the purity with which you loved me. Thank you for the long talks and all the beautiful, irreplaceable memories. I want you to know that I am better for you having been in my life…I am even a better mother to Hadley and Quentin and a better grandmother to Olivia, Nathaniel and Michael now because of you. You changed me. You enriched my life forever. I'm sure you finally get it now that, regardless of the conditions which gave birth to your existence, your Creator never viewed you as a "mistake."

You will not come back to me in this life, but I will come to you. I think often about that day and wonder what it will be like to see you walking toward me again…a thought that is occasionally visited upon my dreams, causing me to wake with lingering melancholy.

I do not know how long I shall tarry here, but I *will* meet you in that better country. So long, my son. So long, my friend. You'll stay in my heart.

PRAYER FOR SALVATION

The most important thing each reader of this book will ever do is to ensure that their soul is saved. Jesus Christ once told His disciples, "Where I go you know and the way you know...*I am the way, the truth and the life.*" (emphasis mine) According to the Holy Bible there is no other name under heaven whereby men must be saved, and every one of us must be born again to see heaven.

Being saved is as simple as ABC:

- Acknowledge you are a sinner
- Believe in your heart that Jesus Christ is the Son of God and trust Him to take the punishment you deserve
- Confess to others that you are a follower of Jesus Christ

Here is a simple prayer to help you get started:

Heavenly Father,
I declare that you are Jehovah God — the only God – who created heaven and earth. I have sinned before you, going my own way instead of following the light that You have sent to me. I come before You,

not to plead my case, but to plead guilty and throw myself upon Your mercy. Please forgive me of my sins; cleanse me from all wickedness. I accept your Son, Jesus Christ, as my Savior. I dedicate my life to learning and following His ways through the study of the Bible, Your Holy Word. Thank You for receiving me and sending Your Spirit to live in me.
Amen.

NOTES

Chapter 4

1 C.S. Lewis, *The Problem of Pain* (New York: Macmillan, 1962), 147.

2 C.S. Lewis, *Mere Christianity* (New York: Macmillan, 1972), 190.

SELECTED BIBLIOGRAPHY

Lewis, C. S. *Mere Christianity.* New York: Macmillan, 1972.
The Problem of Pain. New York: Macmillan, 1962.

To order copies of this book or a copy of the CD of J.D. Morrison's song "Glad You Came Along", please visit www.justicefortruth.org

Contact Information:

Mail: Justice For Truth
P.O. Box 520273
Independence, MO 64052
Email: info@justicefortruth.org
Phone: (816) 674-8350

CPSIA information can be obtained
at www.ICGtesting.com
Printed in the USA
LVHW031742191119
637871LV00004B/565/P

9 781604 773996